Accountable Aid

Local Participation
in Major Projects

Patricia Feeney

**Oxfam
Publications**

cover photograph: San Vincente, El Salvador. Jenny Matthews/Oxfam

Available from the following agents:
for Canada and the USA: Humanities Press International, 165 First Avenue, Atlantic
Highlands, New Jersey NJ 07716-1289, USA; tel. 732 872 1441; fax 732 872 0717
for Southern Africa: David Philip Publishers, PO Box 23408, Claremont, Cape Town 7735,
South Africa; tel. (021) 644136; fax (021) 643358
for Australia: Bush Books, PO Box 1370, Gosford South, NSW 2250, Australia;
tel. (043) 233274; fax (029) 212248
for the rest of the world contact: Oxfam Publishing, 274 Banbury Road, Oxford OX2 7DZ, UK

Published by Oxfam GB, 274 Banbury Road, Oxford OX2 7DZ

JB104/RB/98

Printed by Oxfam Print Unit

Oxfam GB is a registered charity no. 202918, and is a member of Oxfam International.

Contents

Acknowledgements

This book originated in a proposal by the NGO-World Bank Working Group in 1993 to produce a series of studies of the Bank's experience of participation. Oxfam UK and Ireland (to be known from May 1998 as Oxfam GB) decided to assess the level of popular participation in PLANAFLORO, the Rondônia Natural Resource Management Project, which was initiated in Brazil in 1992. Early field work was done in 1994 in collaboration with the agronomist Mario Menezes and the anthropologist Mario Silva. An interim report prepared by Mario Menezes forms the basis of the section in Chapter 2 dealing with the early stages of PLANAFLORO. I am indebted to Brent Millikan, a doctoral candidate in the Department of Geography at the University of California, Berkeley, who wrote parts of Chapter 2, describing frontier expansion in Rondônia and the impact of POLONOROESTE, the predecessor of PLANAFLORO, and also contributed to later sections of the book.

Particular thanks are due to the NGO Forum of Rondônia for their generous co-operation, and to John Garrison, of the World Bank's Brazil office, who was invariably prompt and helpful in answering numerous requests for assistance. In addition, senior staff at the World Bank, the European Commission, and the UK government's Department for International Development (DFID) were kind enough to read early drafts of the case-studies and to offer constructive criticism. Andy Norton and Janet Seeley, both Social Development Advisers at DFID, provided many insights into participatory approaches. Every attempt has been made to improve the analysis and give a fair account of developments and problems encountered in the various projects. Remaining errors are my own responsibility.

Savio Carvalho, Pandurang Hedge, and Nicholas Hildyard offered valuable comments on Chapter 3. I am grateful to the Bugangaizi Settlers for allowing me to recount their harrowing experience of displacement in Chapter 4. In Chapter 5, I have drawn on the analysis of Dr Tom Kenny of the Rights and Accountability in Development

4

Project. The section on the Inspection Panel has been informed by the work of Lori Udall, Dr David Hunter, Dana Clark, and Aurelio Vianna. Nancy Alexander, Alex Wilkes, and Alison Sutton have all at different times provided pertinent information and comments.

There is insufficient space to acknowledge all the Oxfam staff who have contributed directly or indirectly to the report. However, special thanks are due to Michael Bailey, Telma Castello Branco, and Francis McDonagh of the Recife office; John Gwynn, Dr Parasuramman, Roy d'Silva, Gerry Paes, and Vidhyadar Gadgil of Oxfam India; Tony Burdon and Rosemary Kaduru of Oxfam Kampala; and Dianna Melrose, Christine Whitehead, and Anni Long of Oxfam's Policy Department.

Finally, I express my gratitude to David, Edward, and Emma for bearing with great patience the inevitable disruption of our family life.

Patricia Feeney
Oxford, April 1998

Preface

This book attempts to evaluate participatory approaches to natural-resource management by contrasting the different attitudes and methodologies of major development institutions: the World Bank, the European Union, and the Overseas Development Administration (ODA) — the UK government's bilateral aid agency, retitled in 1997 the Department for International Development. It also surveys recent central (and at times conflicting) trends in aid policies. It provides examples of the results of these participatory policies on the ground. The ultimate test of the usefulness of aid interventions is their impact on the lives and livelihoods of people living in poverty. The book's analysis and conclusions are based directly on the experience of local NGOs and communities supported by Oxfam GB in developing countries.

The first chapter provides an overview and assessment of recent trends in aid and sets participatory development in context. Chapter 2 examines the changing attitude of the World Bank to participation through a study of its Rondônia Natural Resource Management Project in Brazil. Chapter 3 considers a conscientious approach to participation, gender, and equity in the UK-funded Western Ghats Forestry Project in India. The consequences that may occur when donors like the European Union fail to implement participatory approaches are analysed in Chapter 4. Chapter 5 outlines the importance of accountability; it examines the development of complaints mechanisms at the World Bank and the obstacles confronting project-affected people in their efforts to obtain a fair hearing and redress from the EU. Chapter 6 charts the extension of participation to wider macro-economic debates and country-assistance strategies. It considers the influence of decentralisation and the challenge of the growing privatisation of development. The final chapter sums up the lessons learned and presents Oxfam's recommendations for accountable aid.

Although this book is mainly an analysis of official aid projects, an appendix contains a critical evaluation of a participatory forest-management project in India supported by Oxfam GB (hereafter referred to as 'Oxfam'). It shows that NGO projects are not necessarily immune from the problems affecting larger, officially sponsored aid programmes.

Views of participation

It may be useful at this point to summarise views of 'participation' taken by a range of major institutions and agencies in the field of social and economic development.

World Bank: Participation is the process through which stakeholders influence and share control over development initiatives and the decisions and resources which affect them.

UNDP: Participation means that people are closely involved in the economic, social, cultural, and political processes that affect their lives.

CIDA (Canadian International Development Agency): Participation is a process whereby individuals and community are actively involved in all phases of development. It therefore involves greater equity and political power.

IDB: Participation in development is both a way of doing development — a process — and an end in itself. As a process, it is based on the notion that individuals and communities must be involved in decisions and programmes that affect their lives. As an end, participation in development means the empowerment of individuals and communities. It means increased self-reliance and sustainability.

EBRD (European Bank for Reconstruction and Development): Participation refers to an organised opportunity for citizens and public and private organisations to express their opinion on general policy goals or concrete decisions made about specific projects and to discuss them with decision makers. It includes the possibility of appealing against government decisions.

DFID (Department for International Development): Participatory approaches take into account the views and needs of the poor, and tackle disparities between men and women throughout society.

UN Committee on Economic, Social and Cultural Rights: Participation has a central role in the development process. The individual is posited as the primary subject of development — with an emphasis on self-reliance, empowerment, and participation. The rights of individuals go beyond the level of mere entitlements to delivery of specific goods and services. Thus the development process is conceived of as being an enabling process whereby structural impediments (both social and economic, on a micro and macro scale) are lifted to allow the individual to define and fulfil his or her material and non-material needs. This is acknowledged in Article 2(i) of the Declaration on the Right to Development, which states 'The human person is the central subject of development and should be the active participant and beneficiary of the right to development.'

Oxfam: Participation is a fundamental right. It is a means of engaging poor people in joint analysis and the development of priorities. Its ultimate goal should be to foster the existing capacities of local, poor women and men and to increase their self-reliance in ways that outlast specific projects. The purpose of participation is to give a permanent voice to poor or marginalised people and integrate them into the decision-making structures and processes that shape their lives.

1 Participatory development: an overview

The demise of many authoritarian regimes at the end of the 1980s coincided with a refocusing of official aid. Since the mid-1980s, donor agencies had been undergoing a series of transformations. Development ceased to be seen in terms of large-scale projects; instead, international financial institutions promoted stringent economic adjustment as the key to growth and poverty alleviation. The failure of structural adjustment programmes to produce the anticipated results led to another change in direction as donors started to call for the modernisation of government systems and structures.

Many of the planning disasters of the past are now attributed to a failure to understand the prevailing economic and political context in developing countries. Ignorance of local conditions leads to a lack of commitment on the part of the intended beneficiaries. A welcome feature of the new approach to development is the focus on the local context and the poverty profile in recipient countries. Never has so much information been collected about and from the intended beneficiaries of aid — the 1.3 billion women, men ,and children who are living below the line of absolute poverty in developing countries on $1 a day. Techniques such as rapid rural appraisal, beneficiary-impact assessments, and stakeholder analyses have generated a mass of documents and guidelines. But how are the data being used? Have they altered the development priorities of donors and governments?

'Participation' as a formula to remedy past failures has been enthusiastically endorsed by most of the world's governments, traditional international financial institutions, and bilateral donor agencies as the most effective instrument for delivering development. This enthusiasm may be related to the fact that 'participation' is a nebulous term which does not impose any specific set of obligations on donors and governments. In truth, while aid levels were high, the absence of local commitment to achieving success or support for a project's aims was frequently disregarded by planners and donor agencies. But throughout the 1980s, community leaders, in partnership with NGOs, began to protest about the damage wrought on the lives and livelihoods of local, usually poor people, by ill-conceived internationally financed infrastructure projects. Their protests, allied to environmental concerns, led to the realisation that strategies for sustainable development had to become more inclusive.

Public participation is a continually evolving concept. It may be broadly defined as an opportunity for citizens and public and private organisations to express their opinions on general policy goals or to have their priorities and needs integrated into decisions made about specific projects and programmes. It allows members of civil society — but particularly the poorest — a chance to discuss development plans with representatives of government and donor institutions. It includes the possibility of appealing against governmental decisions and proposing reasonable alternatives to those in power. It has increasingly been seen less as a particular development tool in the context of specific projects and more as an essential component of the democratisation process, which helps to improve the competence of individual citizens to exercise their right to participate in political life, and also helps to increase the responsiveness and accountability of public administration and government to the public. Increasing public awareness and concern about development — particularly from a social and environmental perspective — has been one of the most important driving forces for increasing public participation.

International human-rights standards have long recognised the right of individuals and communities to be involved in the formulation and implementation of policies, programmes, budgets, legislation, and other activities.[1] The right to participation is clearly connected to all human rights, but is specifically applicable to the realisation of Economic, Social and Cultural Rights. Principle 10 of the Rio Declaration, issued at the United Nations Conference on Environment and Development in 1992, also recognises that environmental issues are best handled with the participation of all concerned citizens. It is recognised that effective participation requires access to information about development and environmental initiatives held by public authorities or donors, or even by private companies.

Oxfam has supported many campaigns for fair treatment for the victims of development: from Brazilian Indian communities, decimated by disease during the road-construction programmes in the Amazon, to tribal people in India, threatened with destitution when dispossessed of their traditional lands to make way for large hydropower schemes. For Oxfam, participation is not simply a way of making aid more effective, but an essential prerequisite for recognising and safeguarding fundamental rights. It is also a means of making aid locally accountable. But if it is to be more than a token gesture, decisions on the scope, nature, and mechanisms of participation cannot simply be imposed by donors or governments; they must emerge from a process of negotiation with local people.

This chapter attempts to summarise the evolution of ideas about participation in the context of the policies of official donors and multilateral development banks. It examines some of the problems and contradictions with the prevailing trends in aid, and assesses the work of official aid institutions and non-government organisations (NGOs) to promote participation.

Trends in official aid policies

Whether development is led by support from Official Development Assistance or by means of private-sector investment, it is unlikely to succeed if it does not incorporate the lessons learned from the campaigns against bad or inappropriate development. High-profile campaigns have publicised the negative impacts of grandiose development schemes that have failed to put people first. As a result, changes in the approaches to development projects have been formally adopted by most major donors, and criteria to inform the implementation of projects have proliferated. The World Bank's Operational Directives, approved by its Board of Directors, are designed to protect the rights of people involuntarily resettled, of indigenous peoples, and of the environment. Environmental impact assessments are required for projects liable to have serious environmental or social impacts. While such standards and guidelines are never fully complied with, they are a measure by which aid interventions should be judged.

The development of standards and good-practice procedures has, of course, been a response to increasing demands from NGOs and citizens' groups for greater openness in development decision-making and for active participation in deliberations that affect people's futures. There has been a realisation that knowledge is power. NGOs have successfully campaigned for the adoption of public-information disclosure policies by multilateral agencies. Consultations with NGOs on policies and projects are increasingly common. An important landmark in the drive for accountable aid was reached in 1993, with the establishment of the World Bank's Inspection Panel — the world's first complaints mechanism for project-affected people. Yet, in spite of these gains, correcting mistakes and redressing the negative consequences that aid interventions may cause to individuals and impoverished communities remains as problematic as ever.

The end of the Cold War

Popular participation is after all democracy at work at the grassroots level.[2]

It is hardly surprising that the impetus for a new aid compact started to be widely endorsed by major donors with the ending of the Cold War. It was not that the concepts of accountability and participation were entirely new in development debates, but that some of the old, less acceptable motives behind development assistance were thought to be a thing of the past. In a speech to the donor community, at a meeting of the Development Assistance Committee of the Organisation for Economic Cooperation and Development (OECD) in Paris in December 1990, Wilfried Thalwitz, a Senior Vice-President of the World Bank's Policy Research and External Affairs Department, set out the new approach:

The end of the Cold War offers an historic opportunity to shape a new, more people-oriented pattern of world security and development....The World Bank has learned from its experience of development that popular participation is important to the success of projects economically, environmentally and socially.[3]

Coupled with the ending of superpower rivalry in the developing world was the unpalatable evidence suggesting that aid transfers had failed to reduce poverty, particularly in areas of the world like sub-Saharan Africa, where, in the view of the World Bank, 'Underlying the litany of Africa's development problems is a crisis of governance'.[4]

Across the world donors came to accept that a pre-condition for successful development efforts was the existence of an appropriate policy environment. Recipient countries were made aware that aid would no longer be automatically provided: in future, flows would depend on their capacity to manage resources effectively. Their record on promoting democracy and respect for human rights would be taken into account. Baroness Chalker, Minister for Overseas Development in the UK government, declared in 1991:

Aid cannot be given in a policy vacuum. Aid ministers are responsible to their own parliaments and people, just as other spending ministers. If we believe our aid is not going to be used effectively to help those for whom it was intended, I am duty bound to ask how its effectiveness can be safeguarded. If it cannot be, I have to question whether it should be spent at all. Our resources are finite and neither we nor recipients of our aid can afford to see them wasted. Some might call this conditionality. I call it common sense.[5]

The new world order emboldened political leaders, and not just those from industrialised countries, to speak out about human-rights abuses and corruption in developing countries. New types of conditionality, requiring governments to instigate political and institutional reform, were grafted on to the existing economic reform packages. But donors' reactions to human-rights abuses have been inconsistent. Since 1990 donors have suspended aid on grounds of human-rights violations and/or interruptions of the democratic process in over 20 countries. Most of these suspensions have been short-term; not all donors agreed to the suspension. It has become clear that the donors are usually willing to act in this way only against the weakest economies, where investments and access to lucrative markets are not at risk. Development NGOs argue that unless transparent criteria are used and proper safeguards put in place, such actions can do more harm than good. There is always a risk that, by enforcing economic sanctions or suspending aid, the donor community may be imposing a collective punishment on an entire population, damaging the interests of the poor, and — as in the case of the sustained embargo on Iraqi oil sales after the Gulf War — sometimes even violating international standards on human rights.

The move to 'good governance'

In response to the limitations of the conditionalities adopted in the 1980s to promote structural adjustment and economic reform packages, the World Bank, whose statutes forbid political considerations to affect its operations, started to emphasise the need for 'good governance' to ensure the sustainability of development programmes. The World Bank defined governance as 'the manner in which power is exercised in the management of a country's economic and social resources for development'.[6] The Bank's traditional concern with sound development management now extends beyond the capacity of public-sector management to the rules and institutions which create a predictable and transparent framework for the conduct of public and private business.

The Bank sees accountability for economic and financial performance as a legitimate and necessary objective of its work.

The Bank's recipe for good governance, which is broadly supported by all donors, includes a range of measures: from strengthening accounting in the public sector to devolving financial power to local authorities. At the policy level, good governance is a method of assisting governments to improve the transparency of budgets and public-expenditure programmes. At the project level, it encourages beneficiary participation 'where appropriate' and the selective use of local NGOs to enhance service delivery. It seeks to promote legal reform, training the judiciary in business and economic laws and encouraging the use of alternative dispute-resolution mechanisms when legal systems are overburdened.

To many observers, however, this definition was unduly narrow. There are signs that the World Bank itself is rethinking the long-term implications of the stringent retrenchment of central government and the rapid introduction of measures to reduce the operations of the State which have undermined the broader conception of good governance. These conditions were heavily promoted in developing countries as part of the World Bank/IMF adjustment loans for debtor countries, in a drive to improve efficiency and cut costs. In its 1997 *World Development Report*, the World Bank acknowledges that recent reforms have tended to emphasise economic fundamentals to the exclusion of the social and institutional basis needed to ensure sustained development and to avoid social disruption. 'Development — economic, social, and sustainable — without an effective state is impossible. It is increasingly recognized that an effective state — not a minimal one — is central to economic and social development'.[7]

Defining participation

Governments which fail to respond to the needs of minorities and the poor do so at their peril.

A key component of the good-governance formula is participation. For donors, participation is still relatively new as an explicit policy. But the Swedish International Development Agency (SIDA) traces its origins to the small-scale community-development projects of the 1960s and 1970s. With the growing realisation that many aid initiatives were simply not sustainable, donors have attempted with varying degrees of success 'to operationalise' participation.[8]

According to the World Bank's original definition, popular participation is the process by which people, especially disadvantaged people, influence decisions which affect their lives. The term 'popular' refers not only to the absolute poor, but to a broad range of people who are disadvantaged in terms of wealth, education, ethnicity, or gender. Participation implies influence on development decisions, not simply involvement in the implementation of benefits of a development programme or project. By 1994 the emphasis had shifted: the term 'popular' was dropped; instead of a focus on the poorest and most disadvantaged, the Bank expressed its concern to work with a wider range of 'stakeholders', defining participation as 'a process through which stakeholders influence and share control over development initiatives and the decisions and resources which affect them'.[9]

In January 1991, the World Bank issued a list of Bank-financed projects 'with potential for NGO involvement' — inviting NGOs to contact Bank staff to explore possibilities for collaboration, though it warned that NGO involvement would normally require the agreement of the developing-country government concerned. In an oddly non-participatory touch, the Bank indicated what role it expected the NGO to play in some projects: from fostering private schools in Madagascar to assisting in the design and monitoring of the implementation of a Natural Resource Management Project (PLANAFLORO) in the State of Rondônia, Brazil.

The Bank announced that it had embarked on a process of 'learning better how to promote popular participation, learning from some exceptionally participatory Bank-financed projects'.[10] While Oxfam and many NGOs questioned both the extent to which the Bank was already promoting participation and the characterisation of some traditional top–down projects as 'exceptionally participatory', the process has produced valuable research and resulted in some positive developments. In 1996, the task-force set up to oversee the work, the Bankwide Learning Group on Participation, produced its report.[11] In a foreword, James Wolfensohn, the Bank's President, claimed that the report presented 'the new direction the World Bank is taking in its support of participation, by recognizing that there is a diversity of stakeholders for every activity we undertake, and that those people affected by development interventions must be included in the decision-making process'. The aim of participatory approaches was 'to produce better results on the ground, improve development efforts and more effectively reach the poor'.

As one of the international agencies advocating wider participation of poor communities in development, Oxfam welcomed this new direction. Despite misgivings about the limitations of the participation on offer, it accepted that 'participatory projects' might provide genuine opportunities to poorer sections of the communities to influence development options and to help them secure the benefits that specific aid programmes or projects were supposed to deliver. Oxfam started to collaborate with interested local organisations in various countries with a view to improving the quality of people's participation.

Since the publication of its report on participation, senior managers at the World Bank have encouraged staff to develop greater awareness of participatory approaches so as to create a greater sense of 'ownership', achieve better results on the ground, and enhance sustainability of Bank-supported operations. The Bank has taken some steps to broaden public consultation in the shaping of Country Assistance Strategies, placing great stress on the use of participatory poverty assessments in which the poor and their organisations are involved in the analytical process. But there are still major gaps: in a study of over 100 Country Assistance Strategies prepared in 1995/96, the Bank found that in only half were gender-related issues specifically addressed — and in most cases very superficially. Similarly the supervision of gender-related activities in projects has generally been weak. While the Bank's commitment to introducing new social assessment procedures should, if properly implemented, help to make gender-linked differences more visible, requirements for new loan operations do not specify the desirability of consulting with women's groups. The Bank in its recent efforts to simplify its Operational Directive on Involuntary Resettlement failed to make any reference to the gender implications of development-induced displacement. The Bank is quick to point out its increasing interest in gathering qualitative information on the needs and perceptions of poor people: of the 22 poverty assessments completed in 1996, 12 were 'participatory'. But there is scant evidence to show that these data are being used systematically to inform lending priorities. The Bank has strengthened the relations between resident missions and local NGO communities and other civil-society institutions. Some 35 NGO liaison staff have been appointed in resident missions, 17 in Africa and 10 in Latin America and the Caribbean. These hold regular briefings for local NGOs on current initiatives and 'listen to' their concerns.

The 'process approach': Britain's bilateral aid programme

In the early 1990s ODA[12] developed what it termed 'a process approach to projects'. Its aid procedures already called for social-impact analysis during sector reviews and at the identification stage of all projects.

Guidelines were issued to ODA staff to help to ensure that the official goals of the UK aid programme — to reduce poverty, to promote the status of women, and to encourage participatory processes (as an aspect of good government) — were built into the wider objectives of each project from the very beginning. While ODA clung to the view that some aid programmes (particularly infrastructure projects) would follow a 'blueprint approach' with fixed objectives, pre-determined outputs and well-structured implementation procedures, it promoted a process approach to projects requiring flexible planning, able to react to developments during implementation. A process approach was particularly recommended when a project's success depended on the participation of beneficiaries[13] and where social issues were predominant. ODA recognised that 'dealing with people and institutions takes time, and outputs can be unpredictable'. It acknowledged that project objectives should not be set in stone, but allowed to develop as the project proceeds and lessons are learned from past experience. It also accepted that, because local institutions and/or communities were involved in the design, appraisal, implementation, and monitoring, the first phase of a project with a process approach should focus on the building of local capacity.

Subsequently, more explicit advice on participation was developed for ODA staff; it sought to distinguish between those with some intermediary role — secondary stakeholders — and those ultimately affected — primary stakeholders, who expect to benefit from or be adversely affected by a project.[14] The advice note warns that the concept of 'villager' as a collective stakeholder is quite meaningless, because the various groups of people living in a village have so little in common. For this reason, ODA acknowledged that, when participation involves a partnership between primary stakeholders and the implementing agency, some kind of alliance or association will need to be established by those sharing a common interest. By 1995, ODA viewed stakeholder participation more broadly as a way of strengthening local ownership of all types of aid activities — in structural adjustment programmes as much as community-level projects. It was a means of encouraging institutional partners to become more responsive to other stakeholders, and, as it openly acknowledged, 'ODA itself has to practise the same principles of responsiveness, transparency and accountability with our aid recipient partners'.

Nevertheless, as with other donors, such guidance is not systematically applied. In 1996, the British government's high-level

Projects and Evaluation Committee approved the Natural Resources Policy Project (which is Britain's contribution to the Pilot Programme to Conserve the Brazilian Rain Forest), co-ordinated by the World Bank, without ensuring that the project team had conducted a prior, independent appraisal. The project, which has a budget of £2,913,051, aims to strengthen State-level environment-protection agencies in four Amazonian States, including Roraima, which has a poor record in terms of respect for the rights of its large indigenous population and support for sustainable development. Although one of the project's stated objectives was to improve co-ordination with civil society, before approving the project ODA had not attempted to consult local Indian community leaders and Brazilian NGOs. No stakeholder analysis or social assessment had been carried out, and the project made no provision to extend the proposed training in environmental management to local people. (After Oxfam raised its concerns about the Natural Resources Policy Project in June 1997, DFID, as ODA was known by then, agreed to undertake a full-scale — if belated — social assessment.)

The European Union

Until relatively recently, the European Union's view of participation was relatively narrow. Of the multilateral institutions, the EU's Directorate General for Development Cooperation (DGVIII) has long led the field with its mechanism for co-financing projects with European NGOs; but in-country its efforts were usually restricted to official programmes, which NGOs were simply called upon to implement. The Commission itself admits that collaboration with decentralised actors only rarely took place 'upstream', since the administrations themselves — the EU or recipient governments — were responsible for the decisions on programme planning and conception.

The framework for development cooperation that is accepted by the members of the OECD is that the role of the donors is to help countries improve their capacity to participate in the global economy and to help people improve their capacity to overcome poverty and be able to participate fully in their societies.[15] This framework was adopted by the OECD Ministerial Council in May 1995 and is seen as a means of not only delivering better aid but also of promoting democracy. The DAC paper 'Orientations on Participatory Development and Good Governance', for example, openly suggests that aid can support transition towards societies which are based on the participation of citizens, the accountability of elected officials, the existence of a free press, an independent judiciary, and respect for human rights.

Decentralisation

Decentralisation is seen as being allied to accountability, efficiency, and community participation. The prevailing wave of enthusiasm for decentralisation has been encouraged by its conceptual compatibility with the decentralised mechanisms of productive-resource allocation associated with free markets. This influential approach considers decentralisation to be the appropriate mechanism for reforming the provision of public goods such as health care, education, and targeted poverty-reduction programmes. However, research shows that devolving decisions about project funding to local governments is not likely, by itself, to promote increased accountability or efficiency. In his study of municipal funds in Mexico, Jonathan Fox notes that 'just as concentrated market power, rent seeking, and other kinds of market failure can block the private sector's promised productive efficiency, authoritarian and/or bureaucratic concentrations of power at local and state levels can prevent decentralization from leading to increased public sector efficiency and accountability'.[16]

The degree to which public services are decentralised affects the way in which government expenditure is translated into human development. In principle, decentralisation is seen to have a number of advantages. One is efficiency: decision-makers who live locally are likely to know more about local conditions, so they should be able to match resources and needs much more precisely. Another is accountability: when decision-makers live and work in close contact with users, they are theoretically exposed to more effective scrutiny and are under greater pressure to deliver the goods. There are also more opportunities for local people to participate in planning services and to pay for some of them through local taxes. But while experience in some countries shows that local governments tend to give a higher priority than central governments to human development, this is not invariably so. Local elites often seize the power that devolves to the lower levels — to the detriment of the poor.

Another obstacle to the potential effectiveness of decentralisation is that central governments have been reluctant to release to the local level either funds or decision-making power.[17] Local governments often suffer from a lack of administrative competence, and weak planning and control systems. In many countries there are manifest dangers of ethnic and religious conflicts, especially when decentralisation involves the control of resources, income, or employment opportunities. Frequently, local councils are not credible institutions for articulating local interests. There is a clear risk — if the diverse character of local governments between and even within countries is not recognised — that donors will simply entrench power in the hands of unrepresentative local elites and marginalise poor communities and vulnerable minorities still further.

A recent study by the Norwegian government confirms this concern. It reveals that donor support has focused almost exclusively on administrative structures and has not paid sufficient attention to political forces and processes at the local level.[18]

Participation and the environmental agenda

The environmental movement has been a powerful influence in helping to reinforce the moves towards participatory forms of development. Before the UNCED summit in Rio de Janeiro in June 1992, approaches to environmental conservation were often insensitive to the needs and rights of local, poor people. Attempts in the 1980s to develop national conservation strategies offered very few opportunities for participation, beyond limited consultation among a few select groups. One of the positive achievements of the Earth Summit was that it helped to dispel some oversimplifications about the causes of environmental degradation: for example, the view that poor and marginal communities were the principal agents of destruction, with their 'obsolete' methods of shifting agriculture, their propensity to have large families, and their perversely destructive encroachment on fragile ecosystems.

Support for the participation of NGOs in development was boosted following the Earth Summit in Rio. Heads of State from 116 countries reached a consensus that urgent action was necessary to meet the twin global challenges of environmental degradation and poverty. They issued a Programme of Action, known as Agenda 21, which called for a new partnership between governments, international organisations, the business sector, and NGOs: each country was to translate the programme of action into a national strategy, tailored to its particular conditions and development objectives. Agenda 21 aimed to open up the national planning process to all affected constituencies, to improve policy-making and increase the stake of those who through joint efforts could make them work. The Earth Summit also helped to give greater force to existing environmental procedures which promoted the principle of participation. Since 1989 the World Bank has had a policy of conducting Environmental Assessments which is supposed to ensure that project options under consideration for Bank financing are environmentally sound and sustainable.

Procedures for conducting EAs were set out in two Operational Directives, OD 4.01 (1989) and OD 4.01 (1991), which require that affected groups and local NGOs be informed and consulted during the EA process. The Directive recommends consultation with these stakeholders at the earliest possible stage, when the project category has been assigned and a draft EA has been prepared. Because information disclosure is a precondition for consultation, the Directive stipulates that 'the borrower provide relevant information prior to consultations'. The information is supposed to be made available in a timely manner and in a form that is meaningful and accessible to the groups being consulted. These requirements were bolstered in October 1993 with the publication of Operational Directive 17.50 on Disclosure of Bank Documents, which gave greater access to EA reports for projects classified as category A or B (i.e. those deemed to have some significant environmental or social impact).

But the results have been disappointing. Recent Bank studies show that consultation often starts only after the terms of reference for an EA have been finalised, preventing NGOs from having a voice in defining the parameters of the EA. Consultation took place at the required stages in only about half of the projects reviewed. A review of EAs in Asian forestry projects found that NGOs felt they had not received information until it was too late to influence either the EA or the project design.

Evidence of the limited impact of EAs on project and programme design is set out in the conclusions of an internal World Bank evaluation report which found as follows:

- Few EAs have any influence on project design, because they are not prepared early enough, which automatically precludes meaningful consideration of alternatives.

- Recommendations of the EAs are often not followed through during project implementation; supervision generally has been lax.

- EAs are often not understood by implementation staff, and in many instances are not even available in project offices.

- Environmental priorities emerging from EAs have not been integrated into the design of advisory services and Country Assistance Strategies.[19]

A more positive finding, however, is that the Bank's policies are slowly helping to change borrower governments' reluctance to engage in consultation.

In comparison with the World Bank, the European Commission, partly as a result of staff shortages, has been much slower to adopt and implement social and environmental guidelines. Although an Environmental Impact Assessment Manual was prepared by DGVIII in 1993, it did not become mandatory until 1996. Those EIAs which were undertaken by the Commission were found to have a number of common deficiencies, including limited consultation with stakeholders and intended beneficiaries. Many environmental projects which started before 1992 were designed without any form of consultation. In most of the financing proposals, gender perspectives have been neglected.[20]

Transparency

A pre-requisite of participation is access to information. Over the past few years, major reforms have taken place which have greatly improved NGO access to information about aid programmes. Concerns about the World Bank's performance came to a head in 1993, when the US Congress withheld authorisation for the release of funds from IDA (the International Development Association — the World Bank's soft-loan window). This led to the introduction, in 1994, of an Information Disclosure Policy. Since then, the Bank has made more of its documents publicly available than any other development institution, through its network of Public Information Centers. There are still limitations: most documents are in English, available on request but very often via electronic mail, which restricts its usefulness to poor people who do not speak English and live far from capital cities. Many other documents, 'such as documents prepared for the consideration or review and approval of the Executive Directors, such as President's Reports and memoranda of the President, remain confidential' — according to the World Bank Policy on Disclosure of Information, March 1994.

Centralisation has been the hallmark of the European Commission's approach to development. As a DAC Evaluation report noted, approval of policies, regional and country strategies, projects and contracting are all centralised in Brussels.[21] Although the situation in some ACP countries is slightly better, on the whole relatively little authority has been delegated to field offices. But problems of access to information have effectively obstructed the nurturing of a culture of participation.

In Oxfam's experience, the Commission's programmes were rarely subjected to rigorous scrutiny. The European Development Fund Committee (which manages EU aid to Lomé countries), for example, did not require impact assessments before making new financing decisions.[22] The concerns of many Member States focused on the need to keep external spending within agreed budget limits, rather than on the quality of the aid on offer. This meant that the Commission was slower to respond to concerns voiced by NGOs about their effective exclusion from the process. This was compounded by the relative lack of interest demonstrated by members of the European Parliament: 'Few decision makers actively sought impact information. EC aid management has been much more driven by resources than by objectives both at the level of the Commission and the level of ACP countries.'[23]

The National Indicative Programmes, NIPs, drawn up by the European Commission and the recipient governments, constitute the largest proportion of aid to the ACP countries. They are five-year agreements which set out development priorities, define the areas of co-operation, earmark projects and programmes, and set a timetable for implementation. However, access to the Commission's preliminary Country Strategy Papers and the final NIP is extremely restricted. As a member of the European Parliament commented, 'So far, indicative programmes have been treated virtually as State secrets. They must become joint commitment programmes to be discussed and concluded with all the operators concerned'.[24]

The institutions of the European Union, with the exception of the European Parliament, tend to be closed to public scrutiny. Meetings have generally been held in private. The demand for greater transparency became more urgent in the early 1990s, when membership of the EU was expanded. Since then, the EU has attempted to increase the democratic legitimacy of its institutions. Two issues continue to concern European NGOs and citizens: the democratic deficit, resulting from the weak role of the Parliament, and the lack of transparency. The declaration attached to the Maastricht Treaty's Final Act called on the European Commission to study the issue of access to information. In response, the Commission and the Council adopted a joint Code of Conduct on Public Access to Council and Commission Documents, providing that 'the public will have the widest possible access to documents held by the Commission and the Council'. The aim is not just to make more information available, but to make it available in a way that provides easy access, in a user-friendly format, when and where it is required. *'The Commission is taking steps to ensure actively that openness and the importance of communication with Community citizens are seen to be part of its political and management culture'.*[25] But the procedures have been controversial, and exceptions overwhelm the rule. There is a broad catch-all provision which allows requests to be refused *'in order to protect the institution's interest in the confidentiality of its proceedings'.*

The British aid programme has gradually become more responsive to outside interest and requests for information from NGOs, but its procedures are still not entirely transparent. Nevertheless there have been major improvements — not least because aid officials recognised the inherent contradiction in insisting on greater openness and transparency from developing countries when ODA itself was not willing to take steps to change its culture of secrecy. However, decisions on the allocation of bilateral aid between different countries and on aid strategies within particular countries have not been open to public debate. Oxfam believes that Country Strategy Papers, which are drawn up every two years or so, should be prepared in a participatory fashion. There is a need to involve NGOs and other representatives of civil society in the recipient country, as well as UK-based NGOs, who are concerned about the integration of cross-cutting issues into the UK's overall aid programme and about its relationship to other donor initiatives. Both groups should be given an opportunity to comment on the strategy before it is approved. Over the past few years, ODA has become more willing to discuss its country plans and its multilateral development policies with NGOs, and to make its evaluations more accessible to the public. New legislation is in preparation giving individuals, NGOs, companies, and journalists, for the first time, a legal right to see official documents and other data held by British government departments. While the proposed Freedom of Information Act will have a 'presumption of openness', exemptions will include communications received in confidence from international organisations or foreign governments. There will also be an Independent Information Commissioner who, in the event that disclosure is refused, can order Whitehall departments and other public agencies to comply or face proceedings for contempt of court.[26]

The role of NGOs in participatory development

One of the major factors driving the concern for participation has been the unprecedented expansion in the numbers of non-government organisations. The number of registered development NGOs based in industrialised countries has grown from 1,600 in 1980 to 22,970 in 1993.[27] There has been a comparable explosion in developing countries. The number of NGOs with consultative status in the UN system has increased five-fold over the last 25 years.[28]

NGOs are regarded as more effective at reaching low-income groups, especially in remote areas, and at working in a relatively participatory way. Two sets of belief drive the increasing preference of donors for funding NGOs: one is that markets and private initiative are seen as the most efficient mechanisms for achieving economic growth and providing most services to most people. Funding NGOs enables donors to achieve two aims simultaneously: to minimise the direct role of governments in the economy, and to provide services in a cost-effective way. NGOs are now used deliberately to replace some services previously regarded as State obligations. While exact figures are difficult to come by, it is probably true that NGOs channel about 10 per cent of total bilateral aid.[29]

The European Commission, through its Decentralised Co-operation: Co-financing with NGOs Unit, has channelled increasingly higher proportions of aid through NGOs. An innovation of Lomé IV has been the expansion of decentralised co-operation that has allowed non-European NGOs and others, including local government, private business, and trade unions, to put forward their own development projects and have direct access to EU. The Commission has seen this measure as a way of meeting local needs and also of reinforcing local capacity. But it has failed to address the problem of the unduly rigid and secretive nature of the system for programming EU aid. In most countries the National Indicative Programme and its priorities have been developed without consultation or the participation of NGOs or other civil-society representatives.

NGOs see themselves as vehicles for democratisation and as essential components of a thriving civil society. There is a tension in the two roles, which many fear will drive NGOs away from their primary mission as agents for social change. While direct donor funding can be an important means of supporting NGO activities, it carries with it a number of attendant risks, including shifting NGO accountability from the communities with whom they work to donors. They become vulnerable to subtle pressures from governments who have to approve direct funding of NGOs. Pressures to co-opt NGOs and make them extensions of the State are apparent in many of the case studies of 'participation' referred to in this report. So too are the increasing efforts being exerted by developing-country governments to regulate the NGO sector which at times seek to constrain in unacceptable ways their legitimate activities and undermine their independence. The World Bank has taken upon itself the task of preparing *A Handbook on Good Practice for Laws Relating to Non-Governmental Organisations*. A draft circulated for comment has caused considerable disquiet, particularly among Asian NGOs. According to the Lawyers' Committee for Human Rights:

The approach that the Handbook has taken...presents opportunities for unwarranted government intrusion into NGO affairs where there is no demonstrated public or governmental interest which warrants protection by government powers. It thus goes beyond the restrictions on freedom of association which international law permits. In this way the Handbook poses a serious threat to the exercise of freedom of association and thus to the ability of the NGO sector to develop independently.[30]

Over the last 10–15 years, NGOs have become more interested in undertaking a systematic evaluation of the impact of their interventions in developing countries. Most evaluations have concerned discrete projects rather than analysing the effectiveness of activities such as institutional strengthening, advocacy, and the promotion of democratic processes.

According to a report prepared for the OECD/DAC Expert Group,[31] the best NGO interventions were innovative and succeeded because they were all grounded in some form of participation with the beneficiaries. But, in spite of a strong articulation of the need to incorporate a gender dimension into NGO development projects, the results have been extremely modest. Similarly, while NGOs are eager to stress the importance of environment, and few NGO projects appear to constitute additional burdens to the environment, most NGOs undertake little environmental analysis at any stage in the project cycle. However, NGO projects which have been put in place specifically to encourage the democratic process or to challenge undemocratic features of society and polity have been remarkably successful.

The report discerns over the past ten years a clear change towards a more flexible and innovative approach to project design, which involves project participants at each stage. While the participation of beneficiaries was a clear factor in project success, the report warns that no amount of participation will overcome weak project management or a hostile external environment.

The DAC study indicates that there is often a gap between NGOs' insistence on the importance of participation and the practice of participation on the ground. Many projects were found to be non-participatory or to manifest a weak degree of participation. Donor-commissioned evaluations generally gave a low priority to participation in evaluation.[32]

Conclusion

There are concerns that despite advances in its approach to participation, the World Bank, in an effort to streamline its procedures and make itself an attractive development partner, is set on reducing the number of days available for project preparation and appraisal. This means that finding time for meaningful consultation will be even more problematic. It is also engaged in a process of simplifying its Operational Directives, which most NGOs see as diluting important development standards which the Bank pioneered. Oxfam welcomes the fact that the EU is supporting moves at the United Nations General Assembly for the establishment of national judicial and administrative channels to give affected parties the opportunity of seeking redress from decisions that are socially and environmentally harmful or which violate human rights. But what about damage wrought on people's lives by aid? In its development cooperation activities the EU has not taken a lead in offering rights to a fair hearing or redress to people whose lives have been damaged by its own projects and programmes.

Oxfam's work on participation has focused on how to weight the balance of decision-making in development towards the needs and aspirations of the poorest communities. Even when participatory channels are available, it has proved very difficult in practice for relatively inexperienced community-based organisations and local NGOs to compete for resources and defend their interests when negotiating with government agencies, politicians or donor institutions. As the following chapters show, unequal access to resources and disparities of wealth lead to unequal power. Inequality, whether rooted in race, ethnicity, or gender, frequently means complete exclusion from genuine partnership and participation.

None of the case studies presented in the following chapters produced completely successful outcomes, but that does not imply that participatory approaches should be discarded as yet another development failure. In two out of the three cases, participation was either somewhat perfunctory or non-existent. These experiences simply reinforce the message that to make participation work requires a lot of effort and commitment from donors, governments, and NGOs alike. The critical elements of a genuinely participatory approach involve good initial planning and early discussions with local people about the priorities and objectives of any proposed projects and programmes. A preparatory phase should allow time to provide training to increase the capacity of NGOs and local people, but particularly those who may be most directly affected, so that they can be actively involved in the decision-making process. Consultation is not simply a token gesture. Extra effort has to be made to elicit the views of women, indigenous people, and other minorities and to protect the interests of children. It requires the setting out of a clear process for participation and decision-making at key stages. The prevailing legal framework should be compatible with a participatory approach. Planners should maintain open communication and take time to explore alternative options put forward by different stakeholders. They should provide feedback on decisions taken, and the ways in which the issues and concerns of local people have been taken into consideration. Beneficiaries should be encouraged to use consultation mechanisms to report on problems. Genuine participatory approaches provide benefits all round. For investors and governments, it helps to secure local consensus and it reduces conflicts, offsetting the problem of delays at later stages. It improves planning, by ensuring that local knowledge and preferences are taken into account. It also minimises risks to the quality of life, health, and the environment. Building into the programme or project mechanisms for joint monitoring, problem-solving, and transparent procedures for dealing with complaints — which allow for prompt redress and compensation to those who may incur losses — will ultimately prove more efficient and equitable. Finally, by increasing people's awareness of how the decision-making process works — who makes decisions; on what basis; how the needs, values and wishes of different groups are taken into account — participation helps to consolidate democracy and promote social justice.

2 The World Bank and the Brazilian Amazon: lessons in participation

In grossly unequal societies, the mechanisms which regulate access to and the exploitation of natural resources tend to benefit the powerful and wealthy more than the poor. Nowhere is this more apparent than in the Brazilian Amazon, where over the past decade conflict over land has resulted in more than two thousand violent deaths, mainly of peasants and Indians. Land distribution is distorted in Brazil, so that fewer than 35,000 people, who have title to large estates, occupy an area equal in size to France, Germany, Spain, Switzerland, and Austria combined. In the northern (Amazonian) region of Brazil, 79 per cent of cultivable land is locked up in unproductive estates, held mainly for speculative purposes.

This chapter examines some of the obstacles preventing the effective participation of the poor and grassroots organisations in large projects. It is divided into three sections. The first discusses the social and political context of migration into the Amazon. The second looks at the problems which beset POLONOROESTE, an early World Bank project in the Amazon, and its legacy in Rondônia State. The final section assesses some of the reasons why the Bank's follow-up project, PLANAFLORO, largely failed — at least in its initial phases — to promote a participatory approach to sustainable development.

Rondônia: State, society, and frontier expansion

Until the arrival of Europeans in the seventeenth century, the present State of Rondônia in the south-western edge of the Brazilian Amazon was home to various indigenous peoples. From the colonial period until the middle of the twentieth century, economic activities generally involved the brutal exploitation of the local population — Indians and the rubber-tappers — and the devastation of natural resources. In the 1960s the construction of a dirt road — later named the BR 364 — linking, for the first time, the State capitals of Cuiaba in Mato Grosso and Porto Velho in Rondônia, profoundly transformed the pattern of human occupation and exploitation of the natural resources in the region. Until then, migration and settlement in Rondônia generally occurred by river transport. BR 364 was part of the strategic plan of the then Brazilian government to encourage the dispersal of the population and open up access to the interior.

After a military coup in 1964, the new government significantly increased the level of federal intervention in Amazonia. The military prioritised infrastructure developments and provided fiscal incentives and credit subsidies to attract private-sector investments into the region. At the same time, the military's preoccupation with national security and the need to occupy the frontier regions of Amazonia took the form of plans to settle 'excess' populations from other parts of Brazil, particularly from the impoverished north-east.

In 1970 the military government launched its Programme of National Integration, PIN (Programa de Integracao Nacional), and established the Instituto Nacional de Colonizaçao e Reforma Agraria, INCRA (the Brazilian Institute for Colonisation and Agrarian Reform), to implement its resettlement programme. INCRA was given responsibility for administering all the federally owned public lands located in a 100-km strip along the federal highways. INCRA was also made responsible for administering lands in the 150-km strip along Brazil's international borders.

Migration and colonisation in the 1970s

In 1970, INCRA began its first resettlement project for small farmers in the then Federal Territory of Rondônia. The opening of the BR 364 and the spread of the news that fertile cheap land was available in Rondônia provoked an unprecedented flow of migrants into the Amazon. According to official estimates, the population in Rondônia increased from 113,000 to about 500,000 between 1970 and 1980; the population was increasing at an average annual rate of 15.8 per cent (compared with 2.48 per cent for the rest of the country). The majority of the migrants were small farmers uprooted by the mechanisation of agriculture and the concentration of landholdings in the centre-south region, who came in search of a better life in Rondônia. But the arrival of large numbers of new migrants in search of land in Rondônia meant that the resettlement capacity of INCRA was rapidly overwhelmed. Increasing numbers of new migrants resorted to the spontaneous occupation of land in the hope that their claims would be eventually recognised.

A map of Brazil, showing the State of Rondônia

Frontier communities

INCRA, as the principal representative of the State in Rondônia, wielded considerable influence. While virgin territory was cleared for agricultural or other purposes at a dizzying speed, the initiatives of FUNAI (Fundação Nacional do Indio, the Brazilian Indian Foundation, a federal agency, responsible for the protection of Indians and their territory) to protect local indigenous communities were extremely weak. Apart from conflicts over land, the Indians suffered the catastrophic effects of diseases introduced by the pioneers.

31

In this period, a significant part of the land under INCRA's administration was occupied by the remaining populations of rubber-tappers and *ribeirinhos* (fishing communities). However, when a colonisation project was set up in areas previously occupied by a traditional group, the maximum that they received by way of compensation was a small rural plot from INCRA, insufficient for them to maintain their traditional way of life. As public land was auctioned and distributed among landowners and other entrepreneurs, the presence of traditional peoples was simply ignored by INCRA, in violation of Brazilian law.

No organisation then existed to represent the indigenous or traditional population of Rondônia that might have been able to defend their interests. Initially the Catholic Church concentrated on forming rural trade unions among the migrant farmers. It is now recognised that, if the forces driving colonisation are to be addressed, then public policies, technological advances, and institutional interventions need to complement rather than contradict each other. Incentives need to be increased to encourage colonists to remain on their existing plots; support for grassroots organisations, rural trade unions, and local NGOs needs to be prioritised. Such organisations help to develop greater social cohesion, secure external support, improve marketing margins, and resist opposing land claims. Government support for social and market infrastructure, especially health facilities, schools, and roads, is essential. But official policies actively discouraged the growth of autonomous social organisations.

Frontier expansion and the environment

In the 1970s the process of frontier expansion in Rondônia and the new private-sector activities (logging, mining, cattle ranching) caused serious environmental damage. The most visible result was the accelerated rate of deforestation. But these activities were encouraged by the military government. In areas occupied by small migrant farmers, serious problems of ecological sustainability arose. Not only was there the problem of the low agricultural potential of much of the land (only 10 per cent of the soils in the State are adapted to agriculture), but also the migrant farmers lacked adequate knowledge of natural-resource management techniques appropriate for the Amazon. Rondônia, like the rest of Brazil, lacked a coherent set of agricultural policies. All these factors created a situation in which the degradation of natural resources became the only rational course in the settlers' struggle for survival. But many farmers abandoned their plots of land, while large landowners bought up their titles (often informally) and expanded cattle-ranching activities. In Rondônia between 1970 and 1988 cattle numbers expanded by 3,000 per cent. There was a tendency among the small farmers, who had been allocated plots of land by INCRA in official settlement projects, to sell these in exchange for cheaper land in new areas of frontier expansion, often in protected areas. They would 'buy' their 'squatters' rights' from land speculators who had already cleared the forest in anticipation that INCRA would eventually grant them title to the property. (This practice continues to be accepted by INCRA as a sign of 'improvement' which strengthens land claims.) These expectations were usually reinforced by local politicians, particularly in electoral periods.

Since the mid-1980s, there have been substantial changes in policy and politics, including the rise of rubber-tapper unions, the ending of ranching incentives, and the curbing of multilaterally funded dams and roads. More political opportunities are now available to grassroots organisations, and new political alliances have been formed, especially among environmental and indigenous rights groups. Despite these changes, the official government policy has largely remained one of frontier expansion.

POLONOROESTE: frontier society and the World Bank

The World Bank entered this turbulent context in 1979, when the Brazilian government initiated negotiations for a loan to finance the reconstruction of the BR 364. The government was interested in paving the highway, whose accessibility was precarious, particularly in the rainy season.

In negotiations with the Brazilian government, some Bank officials raised concerns about the possible negative impacts of a road project in a frontier region. They argued that the paving of the road would stimulate further migration and land speculation, thus increasing deforestation and the invasion of indigenous reserves. Similar concerns were voiced by NGOs, such as Cultural Survival.

In the internal discussions in the World Bank, these concerns eventually gave way to the argument of the project's defenders: that sooner or later the Brazilian government would asphalt the road, with or without World Bank finance, and the best strategy for the Bank would be to fund the BR 364 by means of a regional development package, which would include provision for protecting the environment and supporting indigenous populations. In December 1980, the Bank announced its decision to finance the reconstruction and paving of the highway between Cuiaba and Port Velho, as part of a programme to promote social and economic development and orderly human occupation in the States of Rondônia and Mato Grosso.

With an initial budget of US$1.55 billion, including more than $434.4 million in loans from the World Bank, the Northwest Region Development Programme, or POLONOROESTE (Programa de Desenvolvimento Integrada do Noroeste do Brasil), was created in 1981. The main objective of the programme was the asphalting of the 1,500km highway between Cuiaba and Porto Velho. Other components included improving the network of secondary and feeder roads, consolidation of existing small-farmer settlements, the provision of land tenure and public health services, and the creation of new communities. While the transport sector absorbed over half of the initial budget, less than one-tenth of project funds was reserved for Amerindian and environmental components.[1] There was also to be a series of investments to improve local infrastructure and social services in the colonisation areas: health posts, schools, local roads, and agricultural extension.

An environmental component was included, aimed at establishing conservation areas and environmental protection and research. The indigenous peoples' component proposed the demarcation of Indian areas, as well as measures to support the provision of basic services in health and education. Sensitivities over national sovereignty meant that funding for the Indian component was to be provided by the Brazilian government.

Deforestation

By the mid-1980s, however, the gap between planning and reality was becoming increasingly apparent. Deforestation rates had soared: in 1975, when the first data on deforestation in the Brazilian Amazon became available, it was estimated that the total area of deforestation in Rondônia amounted to 121,700 hectares (0.5 per cent of the total area of the then Federal Territory). By 1980, the area deforested had reached 757,930 hectares (3.1 per cent of the area of Rondônia), and by 1988 cumulative forest clearing in Rondônia had reached some 4.2 million ha, 17.1 per cent of the State's total surface area. POLONOROESTE's planners had expected that migration into Rondônia would increase after the paving of the road, but the rate of arrival of migrants far exceeded official projections. Indeed, between 1980 and 1986, the annual number of immigrants registered at border checkpoints in Rondônia more than tripled, from 49,205 to 165,899.

Migration

This immigration was partially due to the asphalting of the highway, but was also fuelled by a deepening economic crisis.[2] Many migrants moved to Rondônia in search of employment in frontier towns, or for gold prospecting or other non-agricultural activities. The demand for land soon outstripped the government's distribution of small-farmer plots. In 1980 an estimated 20,000 migrant families were waiting to receive land from INCRA; by 1985 the number of landless families was estimated to have doubled. With increasing demand for land from both impoverished migrants and speculators, land values rose, and this further contributed to indiscriminate land occupation. The chaos that ensued threatened fragile eco-systems, natural conservation areas, and Indian reserves. In high-profile campaigns, NGOs put much of the blame for the resulting devastation on the World Bank.[3] Although the World Bank's funding undoubtedly contributed to the increased intensity of migration and the speed of deforestation, its involvement did not ensure that the Indian reserves or conservation units created by the project were effectively protected.

Ruling elites and POLONOROESTE

Insufficient attention has been paid to the underlying political causes of the problems of POLONOROESTE, which have also come to plague the project's successor, PLANAFLORO. The official agencies responsible for implementing the programme had little autonomy of action. They were in thrall to local economically powerful elites who were able to exercise enormous influence over the use of project funds, helping to promote certain project components.

In the 1982 election, programme funds were allegedly deployed in support of particular candidates, all of whom were linked to the government party, which enjoyed enormous prestige as a result of its virtual monopoly of patronage in Rondônia. Many senior officials of implementing agencies launched successful political careers by manipulating investments from POLONOROESTE. Research findings by Brent Millikan, who has made a detailed study of POLONOROESTE, indicate that the government agencies which were funded through the programme provided a useful launch pad for political careers. One of three senators, two of eight federal deputies, two of 24 State deputies, and two of twelve elected mayors were all former INCRA employees.

The former local head of INCRA was elected mayor of the municipality of Ouro Preto d'Oeste, precisely where the first major settlement project, sponsored by POLONOROESTE, was being implemented. Employees of CODARON (the Agricultural Development Company), a parastatal created especially for implementing the Integrated Rural Development Project of POLONOROESTE, also enjoyed significant electoral success, allegedly due to their ability to deploy for their own personal, political advantage CODARON staff and vehicles in the interior, and to raise the promise of infrastructure investments in their campaigns. Four elected State deputies and two of twelve elected mayors in the 1982 elections were ex-employees of CODARON. In the newly created State Assembly this influence was acknowledged in the nickname given to these deputies: the 'CODARON boys'.

The political elite was also able to determine the way in which POLONOROESTE's funds were used. Influence-trafficking was apparent in the selection of sites for the construction of feeder roads, warehouses, health posts, and schools, and in the allocation of contracts. During the lifetime of POLONOROESTE a common practice of both INCRA officials and local politicians was to encourage the 'spontaneous' occupation by migrants of areas with low agricultural potential, or even occupation of protected areas, with the promise that their claims would eventually be recognised. This strategy served a number of purposes: it drew away pressure for expropriation of large and unproductive landholdings; it bought political support from settlers; it facilitated deforestation, because loggers would construct access roads to remote areas for use by settlers in exchange for the 'right' to cut and remove timber; and such occupations could be cited by speculators as proof of intense 'social demand' for land, in order to justify INCRA paying the 'owners' inflated compensation when their property was expropriated.

INCRA recognised deforestation and the planting of grass for pasture as an 'improvement', thereby justifying the recognition of spurious land claims to the obvious benefit of cattle ranchers, land speculators, and local businessmen.

So during the lifetime of POLONOROESTE, the politically and economically powerful elites in Rondônia were able to run the project largely for their own benefit and that of their patronage groups. The participation of the poor, marginalised settlers and traditional populations was conspicuous by its absence.

Suspension

In May 1985, confronted by mounting pressure from NGOs and the US Congress, the World Bank decided to halt disbursement until the Brazilian government took steps to demarcate twelve indigenous areas and protect conservation units. This was the first time that the World Bank had suspended disbursements on social and environmental grounds. The suspension lasted five months, but it helped to ensure that, when the project closed, the remaining Indian areas had been demarcated and that at least some of the services for the settlement projects had been provided. Crucial factors in these achievements were much-improved Bank supervision, the ending of military rule, and the desire of the State government to secure a follow-up loan.

POLONOROESTE prompted a series of reforms in the Bank's lending procedures and the strengthening of its environmental guidelines. In 1987, Barber Conable, the then President of the World bank, described POLONOROESTE as 'a sobering example of an environmentally sound effort which went wrong'.[4]

Unmet needs of poor communities

POLONOROESTE funded some of the State's colonisation projects for migrant farmers, who were allocated 50-hectare plots. But some of the other services which the programme was intended to provide did not materialise. Migrant settlers in Rondônia, like small farmers everywhere, tend to be vulnerable to declining terms of trade. In situations of unusual hardship such as family health emergencies or major indebtedness, the sale of land assets may represent one of the few alternatives available to ensure the short-term survival of the family.

Rondônia, which is roughly the size of Ecuador, currently has around 12,000 families without land. This problem is not likely to be resolved unless the government intervenes to expropriate excessively large land-holdings in the most fertile and productive areas in the State which border the BR 364 road. Because of this situation, the Landless Movement, *Movimento dos Trabalhadores Rurais Sem Terra — MST*, which started working in Rondônia in 1985, has attracted significant local support. The MST is a radical movement in support of landless people which favours direct action: its policy of occupations as a means of forcing the government to provide land has had some success nationally but has also met with violent opposition.[5] In July 1995, for example, a group of MST activists led 600 desperate families to occupy the Fazenda

Santa Elina, in the municipality of Corumbiara in the south of Rondônia. One month later, in a controversial eviction by military police and hired gunmen, eleven people were killed and dozens wounded. Nearly three years later, as with nearly all cases of rural violence, no one has been brought to trial for the incident, although a number of police and rural workes have been charged with responsibility for the deaths. In June 1997, in an effort to curb further occupations by the MST, the Brazilian government announced that INCRA would no longer expropriate lands that had been invaded.[6]

Rubber-tappers

In the late nineteenth century, during the rubber boom, thousands of peasants from the north-east of Brazil were recruited to work in the Amazon, extracting latex used to make rubber. When the Brazilian exports declined, so did the labour force. In the early 1940s, increased war-time demand led to another wave of recruitment in the north-west for 'rubber soldiers'. The rubber-tappers live in isolated *colocaçoes*, little holdings in the forest, close to the rubber trails that they work. Until the late 1970s, rubber-tappers were completely dependent on the owners of the rubber plantations, who controlled the purchase of the rubber and the sale of basic necessities to the rubber-tappers and their families. Rubber-tappers were not allowed to grow their own food or sell their rubber to anyone other than the plantation owner. Lacking information about the market value of their produce and routinely overcharged for things they bought for their subsistence, they were trapped in a system of debt-peonage. In the 1970s government subsidies to rubber plantations were cut and the owners began to sell the estates.[7] In 1990 the Brazilian government signed decrees creating Extractive Reserves in the Amazon, including Rondônia. Extractive reserves (which have received substantial funding from the World Bank through the Pilot Program to Conserve the Brazilian Rain Forest) are conservation areas in which the felling of trees is prohibited, but the exploitation of other natural produce — harvesting nuts or tapping rubber — is permitted to groups of traditional forest-users.

After a visit to the State of Chico Mendes, the leader of Brazil's rubber-tappers, the rubber-tappers in Rondônia started to organise themselves. In 1990 the rubber-tappers' Association of Guajara Mirim was formed with support from Oxfam. A State-level organisation, the Organizaçao dos Seringueiros de Rondônia (The Rondônia Rubber-Tappers' Organisation) — OSR — was also established. Both these organisations have worked to try to secure the creation of extractive reserves and to put them on a sustainable economic footing.

A considerable number of settlers are former rubber-tappers. In many cases they received agricultural plots adjacent to the block forest reserves. They are most likely to practise non-timber forest extraction as a complement to agricultural production. Settlers also supplement their diet by hunting and fishing in the forest reserves. But most fish and game species have declined under pressure from forest clearing.

Indigenous communities

The indigenous population of Brazil is currently estimated at about 330,000 people, who live scattered among 553 indigenous lands, of which 273 have been officially demarcated. The World Bank has long recognised that land is the cornerstone of a secure future for indigenous people, who are highly vulnerable to disease and exploitation, especially in frontier areas such as the Brazilian Amazon. The World Bank has a strong policy, the Operational Directive 4.20 on Indigenous People, which has been approved by its Board of Directors.[8] Under this policy the Bank has supported the Brazilian government in efforts to identify and demarcate indigenous lands since 1981. The Bank also supports projects to strengthen health care of indigenous people in selected regions of the Amazon.

With the destruction of their traditional way of life, Indian communities have become almost completely dependent on erratic and insufficient government subsidies, provided by FUNAI. It is not surprising therefore that the leaders of some communities have accepted the 'generosity' of large landowners and loggers, and allowed them to cut and remove timber or exploit other natural resources such as fish stocks, in exchange for 'presents' — the use of cars, mobile phones, and the other goods, not all of which are evenly distributed among the community members. This has led to many divisions between and among Indian communities.

In Rondônia, the provision of basic services such as primary education is rudimentary. Infant mortality rates are high, and Rondônia has one of the highest rates of malaria transmission in Brazil. Indigenous communities have become increasingly susceptible to malaria. The spread of malaria is largely due to the process of abrupt environmental change, associated with forest clearing and the opening of primitive access roads, all of which have created favourable conditions for malaria transmission. Labour camps are often located next to streams with poor drainage, thus providing an ideal micro-environment for the proliferation of the mosquito vector. In mining areas, old excavations and decantation ponds also facilitate the breeding of mosquitoes.[9]

PLANAFLORO and the struggle for participation

PLANAFLORO, the follow-up project to POLONOROESTE, was a 'child of Rio', in so far as it was publicly launched by the World Bank just before the Earth Summit in Rio de Janeiro in 1992. According to the World Bank's publicity, the project was imbued with progressive ideas: it was sensitive to the needs of the natural environment, 'pro-poor', and participatory. Many other donors and agencies were similarly eager to display their (frequently new-found) green credentials at Rio, and numerous initiatives were unveiled. The Bank was keen to be in the forefront of new lending for environmental projects, in particular to play a dominant role in the Global Environmental Facility (GEF), the main financing instrument for the international agreements signed at Rio. The Bank was also anxious to reassure potential critics that 'the current project incorporates the lessons learned by both the government and the World Bank during the past decade about the necessary ingredients for sustainable development'.[10] Despite this welcome statement of intent, the sequence of events made it hard for the Board of Directors to consider the lessons learned before proceeding with the new project. The highly critical evaluation report of POLONOROESTE was not circulated to the Board of Directors until two months after the $167 million loan for PLANAFLORO had been approved.

The mismatch between the project's wide-ranging objectives and the size of the loan reflected the gradual scaling-down of the project during the negotiation period, itself a product of divided opinions inside the World Bank about its viability. Despite past experiences, the Bank's expectations of the government of Rondônia were unrealistic, given its then existing or foreseeable capacity for implementation.[11] Rondônia, in common with most frontier States, had a poor record on standards in public life, human rights, and equity. On isolated estates, slave labour or debt-peonage flourished; illegal mining in protected areas was openly tolerated; and financial scandals and illicit drug-trafficking were a feature of economic life in the State. Its institutions were far too weak to co-ordinate or enforce the project's objectives effectively, and the situation was made worse by the lack of suitably qualified personnel. Brazil's fiscal crisis added a further complication: the workplans of the implementing agencies were continually disrupted, because the counterpart funds from the federal and State governments were held back. Even at a most cursory glance, Rondônia was not an obvious candidate for the Bank's first experiment in participatory sustainable development.

PLANAFLORO's aims

The Bank identified the beneficiaries of the project as 5,000 to 6,000 Amerindians, 2,400 families of rubber-tappers and other forest dwellers, 900 families in fishing communities and other riverine inhabitants in Rondônia, and a further 52,000 low-income smallholder families. The project document claimed that PLANAFLORO would help rural communities generally by providing improved socio-economic infrastructure and services. Finally, according to the Bank, 'both current and future generations in Rondônia would benefit from actions taken now to arrest deforestation and degradation of the State's natural resource base and biogenetic diversity'.[12]

During negotiations for PLANAFLORO, several NGOs in Rondônia, with support from Brazilian and international NGOs (in particular the US campaigning environmental organisation, EDF — Environmental Defense Fund), raised questions about the new project and its capacity to correct the serious problems that had occurred as a result of the implementation of its predecessor, POLONOROESTE. In January 1990 over 30 environmental and human-rights organisations from Brazil, the USA, and other countries sent a detailed dossier to the Bank's Executive Directors, warning them that the project should not be approved until the Bank had strengthened the mechanisms for implementation and monitoring. In the event, moves to approve the project were disrupted when, in the final days of his government, the outgoing President of Brazil, Jose Sarney, cancelled the Uru eu wau wau Indian reserve — which had been demarcated under POLONOROESTE — in order to placate the demands of local Rondônia politicians.[13] This decision was overturned after pressure from the World Bank.

The incoming Brazilian government admitted its concern about the lack of local participation in the negotiations about the project and its fears for the potential misuse of project funds. The newly appointed Minister of the Environment, José Lutzenberger, who had a first-hand knowledge of Rondônia, publicly insisted that the project could proceed only after wider consultations had taken place with local NGOs. In late 1990 separate meetings were held in Rondônia for the different groups of potential beneficiaries — rubber-tappers, rural workers, and Indians —

which Oxfam (drawn in because of its many years of experience of working with traditional communities in the Amazon) helped to fund. At these meetings local communities were informed for the first time about the objectives of PLANAFLORO. As a result they formulated their demands for participation in the project and a voice in the decision-making processes. The meetings laid the foundations for the formation of the Forum of NGOs and Social Movements of Rondônia ('the Forum'), which was established in 1991 to monitor public policy generally, and PLANAFLORO in particular.

Limited participation

It took an 18-month period of struggle to reach an agreement regarding the official participation of NGOs in PLANAFLORO. In June 1991, the government of Rondônia and the NGOs signed a Protocol of Understanding. This guaranteed NGOs the right to participate in key project commissions related to project planning, monitoring, and evaluation. At the same time the State government committed itself to taking a number of emergency measures to protect the environment and areas allocated for occupation by traditional populations: the Indians and rubber-tappers. The only mention of these agreements in the final project document, the Staff Appraisal Report, refers to NGOs' participation in the project's main management council — the Deliberative Council — and their participation in joint monitoring of the project by an Independent Evaluation Committee (which comprised representatives of the government, the Bank, and NGOs). Although the Forum had received positive assurances from the project manager that the Bank would incorporate the whole of the Protocol of Understanding into the loan agreement, before it was signed in Washington, this was not done.[14] By failing to include as a condition of the loan all the agreements contained in the Protocol of Understanding, the Bank sent a signal to the government of Rondônia that the NGOs and their demands were not to be taken seriously.

In view of these struggles by grassroots organisations, the public invitation issued by the World Bank in 1991 for NGOs 'to assist in the design and monitoring of its Rondônia Natural Resource Management Project' seems more than a little disingenuous. By 1990, the shape of the project had already been decided and the Bank was willing to make only the most minor modifications as a concession to participation. Far from being encouraged to participate, the Rondônia NGOs had had to fight for their place at the table. And they continued to be there on sufferance. Bank missions did not adapt to the new focus on participation, but negotiated exclusively with government officials, by-passing the participatory channels.

A promise of close supervision

Before the project went to the Board for approval, Oxfam had sent a letter to the UK Executive Director conveying the concern of local NGOs that the Bank should not endorse the new project until the State government had complied with the preconditions for the loan agreement. These conditions had been to remove invaders from indigenous reserves and curb illegal logging in protected areas. Oxfam warned the Bank that, unless it took its loan conditions seriously, it would repeat the mistakes of the past.

In response, the Bank sought to reassure Oxfam that it would 'supervise this project very closely, in part because of its complexity and novel design; we believe that the Borrower [the Brazilian government] is committed to this project and will be able to provide counterpart funding on a timely basis'. The Bank insisted that the State government had attempted in good faith to suppress illegal logging and invasions of protected areas, and added that 'with additional resources from the PLANAFLORO project, (it) will be better able to carry out enforcement activities. We will pay careful attention to specific allegations of illegal incursions and will insist on strict compliance by federal and state authorities with their commitments under the legal agreements for the project.' Finally, the letter concluded, 'it is World Bank Policy to encourage popular participation in the assessment and implementation of Bank projects. Our door is always open to NGOs that have a legitimate link to the populations or issues affected by these projects.'[15]

Agro-ecological zoning in Rôndonia

PLANAFLORO's stated aim was to promote a new model of sustainable development in the Amazon. The project was to fund a series of initiatives for the protection and management of natural resources. But the Bank's approach was highly technocratic, and it saw socio-economic and ecological zoning as the key to altering economic behaviour in Rondônia: 'Zoning has already begun to demonstrate its usefulness as a development tool in guiding public investments and discouraging undesirable settlements and resource exploitation in zones considered inappropriate for such purposes'.[16] In its eagerness to conclude the loan, the Bank turned a blind eye to local realities.

The World Bank made the implementation of land-use zoning in Rondônia a main condition in its negotiations over the PLANAFLORO loan. The 'First Approximation of the Zoning' was carried out between 1986 and 1988, without any form of popular participation. The objective of zoning is to prevent the inappropriate exploitation of fragile areas, rationalise land occupation, and ensure better use of natural resources. More advanced forms of zoning take into consideration socio-economic and ecological factors. Zoning was legally introduced by the State of Rondônia by Decree Law 3782, in 1988. In 1991 this was converted into State Complementary Law No 52. All lands in Rondônia were divided into six distinct categories, reflecting their agricultural potential and their importance for biodiversity. All activities in the six zones were to relate to their sustainable development potential.[17] Funds from PLANAFLORO were to support government efforts to implement the zoning.[18]

Zoning was regarded by both the State government and the Bank as a technical exercise. Field surveys were not conducted, poor people were not consulted, and there was an over-reliance on second-hand information, all of which seriously compromised the quality of the First Approximation. Powerful political and economic interests in the State used their influence to maximise the amount of land which be classified as suitable for agricultural and livestock production. World Bank consultants, for their part, did everything they could to maximise the areas classified for conservation and non-timber extraction and non-agricultural purposes. The result was that there were serious errors in the zoning exercise: some areas occupied by rubber-tappers were wrongly included in agricultural production zones. In other cases, areas settled by small farmers bordering the BR 429 road in the Vale do Guapore were classified as conservation zones.

One of the main objectives of PLANAFLORO was to produce detailed studies and maps to correct errors in the first zoning. These would then form the basis for a 'Second Approximation of the Zoning', which would inform and guide all planning decisions in the State such as the legal demarcation of reserved areas and their enforcement. (The Second Approximation of the Zoning was to have been completed by the end of 1993. In fact, despite the importance accorded to them, the technical studies for it did not begin until May 1996 — in what would have been PLANAFLORO's final year.)

The Oxfam Participation Study

In 1994, Oxfam began to study the mechanisms and effectiveness of NGO participation in PLANAFLORO. The Bank had made large claims for the level of participation available to local NGOs and the representatives of poor project-beneficiary groups. Although the Bank later conceded that NGOs had been insufficiently consulted during the appraisal of the project, it nonetheless claimed that PLANAFLORO 'was conceived with an usually advanced blueprint for stakeholder participation in its design and implementation states'.[19]

Oxfam undertook a month-long enquiry which included extensive consultations with Forum members, project staff, UNDP technical support staff, and government officials. Field visits were carried out to enable team members to meet and discuss the situation with the different beneficiary groups, rubber-tappers, small farmers, and indigenous community leaders. The research continued during 1995 and 1996.[20] The initial Oxfam research revealed great dissatisfaction with the project's failure to incorporate grassroots proposals into the planning process. There was also clear evidence of the incompatibility of government policies with the aims of the project, particularly as regards socio-economic and ecological zoning. NGOs complained that, three years after the signing of the agreement with the State government, PLANAFLORO had not developed an effective strategy for ensuring their participation. They were frustrated by the fact that their involvement was limited to a superficial discussion of each implementing agent's annual work plans, which amounted to little more than lists of expenditures. Funds for key components of the project — such as environmental protection and assistance to indigenous groups — were subject to numerous delays, partly because of Brazil's economic crisis. The State government ensured that those funds which did arrive were spent on vehicles, buildings and roads — its traditional priority areas. NGOs which had been excluded from the design and planning phase had to struggle constantly for the right to participate in decisions about the manner of the project's implementation.

A number of problems with the project's overall performance were identified:

- the flouting of the State zoning regulations by INCRA, the agency responsible for issuing land titles;

- failure by the government environmental agencies to protect Indian areas and conservation units, including biological reserves and parks, from invasion and depredation by loggers;

- irregularities in the demarcation of State conservation units (including State extractive reserves);

- failure by FUNAI to demarcate five Indian areas, designated by the World Bank as priority tasks for the first year of the project; and a further failure by FUNAI to implement effectively (with the State health secretariat) the project's indigenous health component;

- the issuing of documents by the State and Federal environmental protection agencies, SEDAM and IBAMA, authorising forest clearance, selective felling, and the transportation of logs to sawmills in protected zones.[21]

These concerns were conveyed directly to the World Bank and were discussed in October 1994 at a meeting of the NGO–World Bank Committee.[22] The initial Oxfam research concluded that PLANAFLORO offered very few opportunities for effective participation by the FORUM and beneficiary groups.

Problems with zoning

In 1992 a State Zoning Commission was established which included government representatives, the private-sector interests (cattle ranchers, loggers, and miners), and NGOs. While this Commission had the potential to play a crucial role in negotiations over any alterations of the zoning, it hardly met and was largely inactive. NGOs reported that they felt intimidated at these meetings.

Given that respect for land-use zoning was critical to the success of PLANAFLORO, it is a pity that the Bank consultants had not found a way of building wider support for it during the preparatory stages. Nor had the Bank helped to promote an understanding of the potential benefits it might bring to Rondônia's civil society during the First Approximation. This left the relatively weak and inexperienced local NGOs and social movements with the unenviable and virtually impossible task of trying to insist that much more powerful political and economic actors in Rondônia should respect zoning and agree clear criteria for any changes to it. For over three years, the Forum struggled to defend the principles of zoning. It also worked hard to reach some accommodation between the different positions of grassroots organisations on the relaxation of the zoning laws. During this period they felt that their efforts had almost no support from visiting Bank missions.

Almost from the beginning, the government of Rondônia took steps to weaken the zoning law. As early as June 1990 the then Governor,

Jeronimo Santana, signed a decree which allowed forest clearing of up to 20 per cent of the area of landholdings, even those situated inside Zones 4 and 5 (classified for non-timber extraction and sustainable forest-management respectively). In June 1994, another Governor, Osvaldo Piana, signed a new decree, which further relaxed restrictions on forest clearing in Zones 4 and 5. Publicly the State government defended these amendments to the zoning law as a response to the needs and concerns of small farmers whose land had been wrongly classified in the First Approximation. But in reality these changes had more to do with the influence of large cattle ranchers and loggers. None of these amendments was discussed with the Zoning Commission. Project technical staff and the Forum agreed that the way in which PLANAFLORO was being implemented was undermining the whole concept of zoning in Rondônia.

Spontaneous land occupation

One of the major problems denounced by the Forum was the failure of INCRA to respect the State zoning regulations in its land-titling operations. According to Amnesty International and Human Rights Watch, the practice of issuing false land titles is notorious in Brazil. Obtaining land through fraud is known as *grilagem*. Peasants and rubber-tappers often claim that, although they may have *bona fide* rights of tenure, which are not yet registered in title deeds, they are forced off the land by speculators or powerful landowners, who may have obtained titles fraudulently.[23]

One of the conditions for loan effectiveness was the signing of an agreement between the government of Rondônia and INCRA to ensure that land-regularisation policies and practices in the State were to be consistent with the objectives of sound forest-protection and management, and satisfactory to the Bank.[24] Failure by INCRA to support settlers and consolidate their occupation in the original colonisation areas in Zones 1 and 2 meant that many, faced with insuperable difficulties, sold their plots of land to large landowners, who then acquired control over most of this fertile region and expanded cattle ranching. This then left rural workers with no other choice but to demand access to new land in more remote areas. The initial stages of frontier expansion are usually portrayed as an essentially 'spontaneous' process, in which landless migrants and land speculators invade previously unoccupied public or private space. On this view, projects like PLANAFLORO help government agencies to instil order, settle land disputes, and promote agrarian reform and colonisation activities. But research reveals a more complex picture, in which land speculators target areas, often buffer zones, surrounding reserves. Land speculators move in and informally demarcate plots for 'sale' to urban residents. INCRA appears to have tolerated this informal land market. An Oxfam consultant reported how he came across men from a local town illegally felling trees with chainsaws in an area that directly affected the rubber-tapping trails in the forest reserve. When challenged, they claimed that local INCRA officials had told them that the agency was soon going 'to cut the land', granting recognition to squatters' rights.[25]

Owners of large estates have also expanded their holdings, using hired labourers to clear and demarcate forest lands, which are then annexed to their property. It is not uncommon in Rondônia for INCRA then to expropriate the encroached area for the purposes of land reform, paying inflated compensation payments to the 'landowners'. The process of land speculation in Rondônia has clearly been encouraged by the expectation that INCRA would eventually issue land titles for 'spontaneous occupation'. In fact there is evidence that the local INCRA office connived at these 'spontaneous occupations' by issuing documents entitled 'Request for Authorisation of Occupation'. Buyers had no doubt that the agency would later grant them official title deeds. Loggers moved in and built access roads for the purchasers in exchange for timber-extraction rights. They quickly removed most of the valuable timber.[26]

In June 1997, the Federal Government announced measures to curb excessive levels of compensation being paid to owners of properties which had been expropriated.[27]

Flawed institutional mechanisms

NGOs' participation in the project-management councils had no concrete results, because they were excluded from the process of drawing up and monitoring the work programmes. There was a general concern expressed by all the NGOs that they were simply being used to give legitimacy to the actions of the government, which often directly contradicted the objectives of the project.[28] The NGOs felt that, given the direction the project was taking, it was becoming impossible for them to continue co-operating with it. An analysis by the Oxfam team upheld the NGOs' complaint that the work programmes of each of the official implementing agencies were not co-ordinated and that they were little more than a jumble of disparate activities.

The procedures of the State Deliberative Council provided a telling example of how popular participation had been diluted in PLANAFLORO. On the few occasions when the Council met, the sole purpose was to obtain formal approval of the annual work plans. NGOs, which had no say over the direction of these plans (they had inadequate advance warning of such meetings, and documentation was frequently not provided until the last minute), found themselves in the position of having to passively endorse the plans and so legitimise the flow of financial resources to the various government agencies involved. But while the official institutions of PLANAFLORO that included NGO participation were emptied of content, major decisions related to the programme were made in isolation by a small group of high-level government officials. The officials would then take arbitrary decisions, such as to reduce the limits of conservation units to placate political and economic interests in the State. The NGOs attempted in vain to warn the Bank about the political interference within the executing agencies, the use of PLANAFLORO funds to contract staff with no appropriate qualifications, and the worrying lack of transparency in the procedures for bidding and awarding contracts.[29] No action was taken. Part of the problem was that the World Bank missions dealt solely with the government and excluded the Forum from negotiations.

One of the instruments available to NGOs to correct distortions in the implementation of PLANAFLORO should have been the Independent Evaluation Committee, the IEC. The IEC was to monitor the government of Rondônia's environmental policies and practices, respect for the zoning laws, and the performance of various project components. But the IEC was convened only during the first year of the project. The Bank claimed that the IEC was unable to produce a final report, but failed to note the difficulties it had encountered. Its work was hampered by a severe lack of logistical support; there were blatant attempts at political interference: members of the IEC complained that they were under pressure to 'tone down' their report; and, finally, when the draft report was submitted, there was a marked lack of interest, on the part of both the Bank and the government of Rondônia, in its findings. The IEC was not reconvened.

In response to a questionnaire prepared by the Oxfam team, over 70 per cent of the members of the Forum expressed dissatisfaction with the form of participation in PLANAFLORO; 95 per cent found participation extremely difficult; 45 per cent expressed satisfaction with the activities of the NGOs. All wanted major changes in the project and the mechanisms for participation.

Interviews with the beneficiaries — most of whom understood very little about the project — made it apparent that delays in the implementation of key components of the project were having a damaging effect on their livelihoods and well-being. These discussions also cast light on the ways in which government agencies, such as the government's rural extension service, EMATER, were able to determine the use of project funds. Clearly, participation is meaningless when the available institutions and mechanisms are controlled by the State, or subject to political domination by local elites.

The views of rural workers

While there was a marked interest among the rural workers in adapting what they produced to suit the conditions in Rondônia, they were frustrated by the absence of any appropriate government support and training: *'A lot of us here know that cutting trees and burning more of the forest will only make us poorer. The problem is that we farmers have never been given information about how to work our plots of land.'*[30] The rural workers had a vague idea that the project should have facilitated their access to rural credit, but none of them had any knowledge about the work plans drawn up supposedly on their behalf by EMATER for 1993 and 1994: they had never been consulted about what they would have liked to get out of the project. Ignoring the existence of established rural trade unions or local co-operative associations, EMATER had created new 'associations' that it could control. Not only did this allow EMATER to carry on providing its conventional rural services, most of which had little relevance to the needs of small farmers, but it also obstructed the formation of genuinely representative and independent local associations. In one municipality, Ji-Parana, 20 out of a total of 30 associations had been created by EMATER. The Executive Secretaries of many of the EMATER associations had previously been employed by the rural extension service. EMATER ensured that the rural services were directed largely to their favoured associations. The settler farmers were not consulted about the activities to be undertaken in PLANAFLORO's agricultural component, which were focused on the production of cash crops. EMATER paid little attention to the need for subsistence production. In Rondônia a total of 50 elected officials, including local councillors, mayors, and State deputies, had previously worked for EMATER. This helped to ensure that the available rural credit was directed towards a limited number of municipalities.

The main agricultural policies pursued by the State continued to promote large-scale monocultures which were inimical to the objectives of PLANAFLORO. EMATER, instead of promoting inter-cropping and mixed-species plantations, as envisaged by PLANAFLORO's agro-forestry component, continued to implement monocultures like cotton and citrus. The type of production favoured by EMATER was capital- and labour-intensive and required expensive chemical inputs, all of which made it unsuitable for small farmers. In Ji-Parana the income from cotton barely covered the costs of production. The use of pesticides not only damages the environment, but, when applied inexpertly, can be harmful to humans and livestock. Despite this, no training had been given to the communities involved in cotton production.

The views of indigenous communities

Indigenous leaders complained that Indian reserves were being left unprotected and, as a result, overrun by loggers, invaders and prospectors. The boundaries of already demarcated reserves were supposed to have been renewed with PLANAFLORO funds in the first year of the project, but in mid-1994 this work had not even begun. The majority of these areas had been invaded by logging companies. The Indians pointed out that the government — in violation of the loan agreement — had failed to demarcate in the first year of the project five indigenous areas considered to be priorities: Sagarana, Rio Guapore, Rio Mequens, Karipuna and Massaco.

Delays in hiring specialised personnel required to implement the indigenous health-care component were causing immense harm. Local health workers told Oxfam that entire Indian villages were infected with malaria. After one year, almost nothing had been done to set up and equip mobile health teams and provide basic pharmacies in Indian villages. The few mobile health teams which were working were unable to visit all Indian areas, and they often lacked basic equipment such as microscopes.

Despite the potential importance of alternative production projects within Indian areas, FUNAI was promoting these activities with PLANAFLORO funds in a questionable manner. Projects were drafted by FUNAI and EMATER technical staff without any analysis of their viability and sustainability in economic, cultural, and environmental terms, and without taking into consideration traditional forms of production among indigenous communities. Nor were the projects submitted to the sectoral planning committee on indigenous affairs for prior approval.

None of the operations envisaged in the 1993 work plan to protect isolated Indians had been implemented. FUNAI made little attempt to strengthen the team engaged in contacting isolated Indians. Senior FUNAI officials even denied the presence of such groups, despite the evidence produced by field surveys. NGOs working with Indians expressed particular concern about the region bordering the BR 421 road (illegally constructed against the zoning laws and with PLANAFLORO funds), linking the towns of Vila Nova do Mamore and Ariquemes. The road would facilitate the exploitation of the area's natural resources. The NGOs wanted the government and the Bank to act rapidly to curb the activities of loggers already operating in areas inhabited by isolated Indians.

The views of rural women

PLANAFLORO has never had any special focus on the needs of women in Rondônia. A limited survey undertaken by Oxfam among rural women showed considerable agreement between women and men about measures they believed were required to improve the quality of their lives. More than half the women interviewed felt that they did have reasonable opportunities to participate in their local trade unions or co-operative associations. The great majority complained that they had received very little information about PLANAFLORO. Female-headed households identified the lack of access to land and rural credit as the main problems. But in addition they wanted ways of selling their agricultural surpluses at a reasonable price, which meant improving their access to local markets. All the women interviewed wanted more attention to be devoted to their training needs, so that they could take a more effective part in the rural trade-union movement. they wanted access to advice on women's health and information about their legal rights. All wanted to ensure that their children had better access to health and education.

The views of rubber-tappers

The rubber-tappers were the best-informed of all the beneficiary groups about the aims of PLANAFLORO, which is a reflection of the quality of support they had received from local NGOs. While they were enthusiastic about the potential of the project, they were disenchanted with the failure of implementation. According to Ze Maria, one of the leaders of the rubber-tappers, 'The name has changed, but they're serving up the same old dish. The government isn't using the money to create reserves, only to help the landowners.'[31] Rubber-tappers told Oxfam that they had had only one meeting in 1992 with World Bank representatives about the project. In 1993, after pressure from the rubber-tappers' leaders, members of a World Bank mission, without giving OSR any advance warning, visited the Rio Ouro Preto Extractive Reserve by helicopter. (Usually the World Bank missions simply flew over the area without landing.) They expressed concern about delays in the demarcation of conservation units such as the Rio Cautario Extractive Reserve, which according to the loan agreement should have been created by September 1993.[32] The uncertain legal status of the reserves encouraged intrusion by logging companies and land speculators, which in turn undermined the livelihoods of the rubber-tappers. (Rio Cautario was created in July 1995, shortly after the submission of a Request for Inspection. Its boundaries were reduced to accommodate those who had staked claims to land inside the reserve while its status was unresolved.)

Despite all these problems, the NGOs believed that PLANAFLORO had the potential to make a significant contribution to promoting sustainable development in Rondônia. They conceded that not all the problems associated with the project were the fault of the Bank, and that the situation was aggravated by the economic crisis in Brazil. This meant that disbursements of funds for the project were subject to prolonged delays. The interim findings of the Oxfam study, which was widely circulated and discussed with the NGOs, project staff, and Bank officials, clearly showed that for PLANAFLORO to succeed, something more radical than the minor adjustment to the formal participation mechanisms (envisaged by some Bank staff) would be required.

Relations between the government, business interests, the Bank, and civil society had to be transformed, and greater efforts would have to be made by the project, through public education campaigns and other means, to change local attitudes to the environment and to address the immediate needs and priorities of the poor.[33]

The findings of the Inspection Panel

In June 1995, the NGO Forum of Rondônia requested an investigation of the project by the Bank's newly created complaints mechanism, the Inspection Panel. After a series of reviews and visits to Rondônia, the Inspection Panel concluded that PLANAFLORO's design had not incorporated the lessons from POLONOROESTE. In several critical respects, the Bank had failed to supervise PLANAFLORO effectively and to enforce the implementation of key activities. There was a complacent reaction to repeated defaults on covenants under the loan.

Over the first two or three years of the project, the situation for many intended beneficiaries by and large deteriorated. One important lesson from POLONOROESTE, not reflected in PLANAFLORO's design, was that the physical demarcation of conservation areas and Indian reserves is a necessary, but not sufficient, condition for their protection. The Bank's Operations Evaluations Department Report 10039 observed that 'Financial disincentives and strong enforcement capacity to prevent and punish invasions are also required'.

Perhaps the Bank's most serious fault was that it did not insist on proper accounting records. During the project's first three years, the government of Rondônia did not submit yearly audit reports, as required under the loan. The long-overdue external audit (which was conducted in 1996) for the first three years reported that over $11 million in disbursement had not been properly accounted for. (The Bank's internal Auditor is to carry out an internal review.)[34]

Conclusion

Undoubtedly the most senior levels of the Bank were genuinely concerned about correcting the problems associated with POLONOROESTE. This led to PLANAFLORO's emphasis on over-sophisticated and technocratic environmental solutions which far surpassed Rondônia's institutional capacity. Then, after complaints from NGOs about the top–down approach, a few concessions were made and PLANAFLORO was fashionably restyled as a participatory project. But little thought had been given to how this might function. The government of Rondônia, for its part, with few other sources of revenue, needed the influx of new project funds. PLANAFLORO was a means of continuing if not correcting what POLONOROESTE had begun. There was no commonality of interests to keep PLANAFLORO on course. It is ironic that those most committed to PLANAFLORO's aims — the NGOs and the intended beneficiaries — became its fiercest critics.

Postscript

The problems that bedevilled PLANAFLORO were not, of course, all of the World Bank's making. Gold and cassiterite mining unexpectedly arose as a major alternative to agriculture, leading to a type of damage with which PLANAFLORO was not designed to deal. But at times the World Bank has evinced little understanding of the difficulties confronting small NGOs in remote areas with limited experience of democratic processes. Initially, at least, their need for some basic technical training (to enable them to monitor budgets and work plans) was largely ignored by the project; it was Oxfam and WWF who tried, with limited success, to correct this imbalance by funding advisers to work with community-based organisations and the Forum. (Between 1994 and 1997, Oxfam allocated $341,060 in grants to support local organisations in Rondônia.) Participation was a belated and, in some quarters, an unwelcome addition to PLANAFLORO's original design. The Bank is right to remind critics of the project that its investments in Rondônia have had some positive results: more than half of the State has been set aside for conservation as Park land, indigenous reserves, and extractive reserves. This is the largest proportion so allocated in any State in Brazil, with the possible exception of Roraima. Oxfam, the Rondônia Forum, and the beneficiaries themselves all recognise that without World Bank support none of this could have been achieved. The challenge is to find a way of ensuring the future sustainability of the Bank's investments. It could be argued that, in the absence of any effective policing and enforcement capacity, without efforts to mobilise the population behind conservation efforts, and in the absence of any real economic alternatives, the ambitious zoning policy which theoretically placed so much land off-limits might have been counter-productive. Did fear of losing access to Rondônia's forest resources actually accelerate the unsustainable exploitation of its natural resources?

Since 1996 the World Bank, recognising that PLANAFLORO has been failing to meet its key objectives, has made concerted efforts to improve the project's performance. With only eight months left before the PLANAFLORO's formal closing date, the Bank hired external consultants to carry out a rapid mid-term review of the project. The speed with which the review was conducted meant that some areas were dealt with superficially, and, in the case of the critical Indian component, some were omitted altogether. NGOs were not involved in the review, despite the Bank-sponsored consultations on ways of improving their participation in the project. The Bank apparently felt that, as stakeholders, the NGOs would lack objectivity. The report of the mid-term review was presented at a seminar in Porto Velho in June 1996. The report did not allocate blame for the project's poor level of implementation, but instead sought to forge a new consensus between the State government, local businessmen and ranchers, and the NGOs, based on what the Bank felt was a less ambitious but workable restructured project. To some exten·

the review achieved its purpose. Agreement was reached to extend the project for another two years, on condition that its management structure was streamlined, that the number of separate components was reduced, and that responsibility for providing community-level services was decentralised to the NGOs and local municipalities.

NGOs now have a stronger formal role inside the project: helping to develop and administer small-scale community projects. Funds have also been allocated to enable the NGO Forum to monitor implementation of the overall project. But there is a real danger that the relatively small and over-stretched NGO community will not be able to carry out these multiple roles. Nor are there many hopeful signs that the State or Federal governments are really committed to PLANAFLORO's vision of sustainable development. While the World Bank seminar on the future of PLANAFLORO was taking place, the State Legislative Assembly passed an amendment further diluting the State's zoning law. More recently, in January 1998, the Brazilian Congress passed a law — the Environmental Crimes Act — which for the first time gives Brazil's environmental agencies authority to enforce the law. But the Brazilian President, under pressure from ranchers and industry, has agreed to veto critical parts of the legislation, and has thus substantially weakened it. Just before the new law was passed, the government released figures derived from an analysis of satellite images which show that the greatest remaining tropical forest in the world continues to shrink. In 1995, partly as a result of dry weather and the economic boom, an all-time record of 29,000 sq km of forest (11,200 square miles — an area about the size of Belgium) was cleared. The consequences of this devastation are most evident in Rondônia. According to just-completed estimates by the Remote Sensing Laboratory at the State Environmental Secretariat, the cumulative area deforested in Rondônia increased from 3,981,313 hectares in 1993 (17 per cent of total land area) to 4,873,143 hectares in 1995 (20 per cent of the State's total surface area). The total area deforested in Rondônia between 1993 and 1995 (891,830 hectares) demonstrates a dramatic increase in annual clearing, especially in relation to the 1990-91 period. Official estimates for 1997 indicate that by the end of 1997 the total area deforested is likely to amount to 23 per cent of the State's territory. It is also clear that, despite considerable World Bank support to improve environment-monitoring capacities in Rondônia, this has not been accompanied by similar efforts at the local level to use the available data, such as the burning reports, available from the Remote Sensing Laboratory, for the purpose of monitoring and enforcement. In the absence of political will, these reports end up as mere historical records of environmental destruction.

If the lessons of PLANAFLORO have been learned, Oxfam believes that the World Bank, in partnership with NGOs, can help to reverse this situation. The Bank should continue its policy dialogue with government and industry, but not at the expense of neglecting efforts to build local capacity. More could be done to mobilise local people — giving them accurate information about the impact of deforestation — through media campaigns; and specific interventions to address the practical needs of poor farming communities and indigenous communities should be increased. As subsequent chapters will show, where donors or external institutions make a conscious and sustained effort to improve the quality of participation, the achievements of specific projects and programmes are more securely established.

3 Gender, equity, and exclusion in the Western Ghats

No society treats its women as well as its men ... Gender inequality is strongly associated with human poverty.[1]

The lives of many women in developing countries are defined by gross injustice, poverty, and hardship. Isolated from economic opportunities, these women are unable to make their contribution to the development process, and their particular needs and perspectives remain largely ignored. In Oxfam's experience, the most successful development assistance to women entails the recognition and protection of their rights. The reason is simply that gender-linked inequality is an obstacle to the improvement of the position of women. Development programmes or projects which neglect the issue of discrimination end up by reinforcing it. The effects of aid are different for women and men beneficiaries not simply because of their sex, but as a consequence of institutionalised gender-related discrimination. From the mid-1980s donor agencies have made increasing efforts to gather gender-specific data and to document gender-linked discrimination. They, have, however, been less successful in integrating a gender-based perspective into all their programmes and projects.

The OECD Guiding Principles require donors to secure the commitment of recipient countries to the rights of women. In particular, they require recognition of the right of women 'to participate in the process of development and to benefit from its fruits'.[2] In the past, some donors began to focus on women's projects which were designed explicitly to benefit women, but these were based on the erroneous vision of female beneficiaries as a homogeneous group. This reductionist approach tended to reinforce sex-based distinctions, rather than trying to diminish their negative consequences. Women's projects were all too often a matter of problem avoidance: addressing the *consequences* of gender-linked discrimination, instead of tackling discrimination itself. Such projects failed or sidelined women to gender-segregated activities, which served only to entrench obstacles to their participation in development.

This chapter looks at best practice in participatory natural-resource management. Whereas PLANAFLORO was a participatory project in name only, the Western Ghats Forestry Project in India, financed by Britain's Overseas Development Administration (ODA), is an example of a genuine attempt by a bilateral donor agency to promote community forestry and to place special emphasis on the needs of poor, local women users. By contrast, the European Union's Natural Forest Management and Conservation Project in Uganda (see Chapter 4) adopted a rigorously protectionist approach, predicated on large-scale evictions, which ended by excluding poor communities from forest areas and their sole means of earning their livelihoods. In the latter case, those who suffered most from a project, which perpetuated an outdated model of forest conservation, tended to be female heads of households and widows.

Women, poverty, and the environment

In India the effects on the poor of State control of the forests, and the appropriation of these resources by private interests, have been the subject of numerous studies. The underlying causes of environmental degradation vary from place to place and depend to a large extent on the class and sex of those who rely on these resources for their living. Unsurprisingly, households located in areas vulnerable to environmental degradation are likely to be most at risk; and within these areas the effects of deforestation are especially severe for poor households, because of their dependence on communal resources. In India an estimated 30 million or more people depend wholly or substantially on non-timber forest produce (NTFP) for a livelihood.[3] These sources are especially critical during lean agricultural seasons and during periods of drought and famine.

Some donors have become more aware of the fact that focusing on the class-related significance of communal resources provides only a partial picture. There is also a critical gender-linked dimension: women and female children are all too often the ones most adversely affected by environmental degradation.[4] In India, as in other parts of the developing world, there is a pre-existing gender-based division of labour. It is women in poor peasant and tribal households who do much of the gathering and fetching from the forests, village commons, rivers, and wells. Women carry a significant responsibility for family subsistence and are often the sole economic providers. But women's ability to fulfil this responsibility is more constrained than is men's, because of inequalities in access to productive and subsistence resources. In many parts of India there is a systematic anti-female bias in the distribution of subsistence resources within rural households, reflected in a range of indicators such as morbidity and mortality rates. There are also significant inequalities in men's and women's access to productive resources, other assets, and income-earning opportunities. In South Asia the majority of poor women depend on agriculture for their livelihood. But few women own or control land, which impedes their efforts to ward off poverty for themselves and their families. Lack of access to land is especially critical for female-headed households. Many factors obstruct women's access to land. In some cases inheritance laws favour men; in others it is social prejudice, religious custom, or cultural practices which debar women from claiming and managing land.

Women also occupy a systematically disadvantaged position in the labour market: compared with men, they have fewer employment opportunities, enjoy less occupational mobility, and receive lower levels of training and lower payments for the same or similar work. They also face much greater seasonal fluctuations in their employment and earnings than do men: in most regions women generally have less chance of finding employment in the slack seasons. Oxfam has found that poverty accentuates inequalities between men and women, and it is women who are often the most vulnerable in times of adversity.

The failure of 'social forestry'

In 1989 the UK government decided to earmark £100 million of the British aid budget to finance activities to protect the environment, particularly tropical forests. Shortly afterwards, the governments of India and Britain agreed on a joint programme of co-operation in the forestry sector (OFI and KFD 1990). In 1988 the Karnataka Forest Department (KFD) had submitted a proposal for an extensive afforestation project throughout the Ghats districts of the State. But this proposal did not fit well with the prevailing vogue among donors for the promotion of participatory common-property regimes for 'common pool resources'.[5] Gradually ODA reshaped KFD's proposal into a community-based management project.

With the Western Ghats Project, there was a conscious attempt by British ODA (now DFID) to learn from the mistakes of previous social forestry projects. In the 1980s ODA and the World Bank had jointly funded the Karnataka Social Forestry Project. It had two major components: farm forestry on private lands, and community forestry on village commons and government wastelands. It aimed to involve communities in planning and decision-making, and it claimed to have made special provisions for the poorest sections of the communities. The objective was to increase the supply of fuelwood to rural and semi-urban areas. Firewood is the single most important source of domestic fuel in India. Much of it is gathered for free and not purchased by the poor. In recent years, there has been a notable increase in firewood-collection time. With the loss of village grazing land, fodder shortages are being felt even more acutely across large parts of India. These factors have resulted in the lengthening of the working day of women (which averages 10–12 hours a day) and of children. The decline in gathered items from forests and village commons has also directly reduced women's incomes. The erosion of other sources of livelihood means that, for many years now, selling firewood has become a common coping strategy for women in some regions. They are called *headloaders*, and they barely manage to eke out a living from this laborious work.

ODA saw the Karnataka Social Forestry Project (KSFP) as poverty-focused.[6] But the KSFP failed to achieve its intended benefits for the landless. This was largely because village commons, especially grazing areas, were planted exclusively with one type of tree, a form of monoculture which met the needs of Karnataka's pulp industry, but completely neglected the fuel and fodder needs of the villagers. In many cases, where commons had been planted, no village meetings had been held and, in the few exceptions where they had taken place, they were dominated by the wealthier groups. When the KFD proposed a second phase for the Social Forestry Project, it was strongly opposed by a coalition of local NGOs, FEVORD-K — the Federation for Voluntary Agencies for Rural Development in Karnataka — which was established in 1982 to provide an umbrella advocacy organisation to influence government policy and procedures. Many of its members are supported by Oxfam.

Western Ghats Forestry Project

The Western Ghats extend along the west coast of India, in the State of Karnataka. Over the years, the forest has suffered from excessive exploitation: infrastructural development, power projects, and commercial logging have all taken their toll. There is also considerable pressure on resources from the growing local population. One of the main criticisms that Oxfam and FEVORD-K made about KFD's original proposal for the Western Ghats was its failure to ensure popular participation. Rural people were regarded only as a source of labour and as beneficiaries who might receive certain privileges. For the KFD, the poor were not seen as active participants in the implementation of the project (FEVORD-K 1990).

A map of India, showing Sirsi and Shimoga in Karnataka State

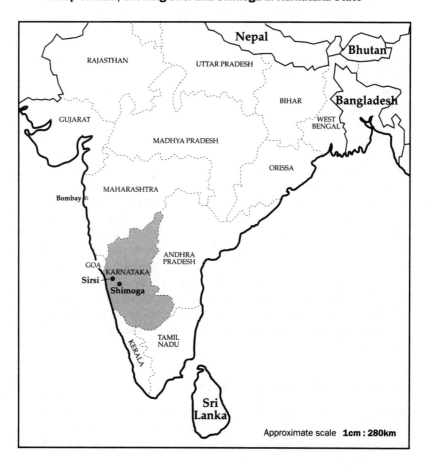

ODA was under pressure to sponsor environmental projects, and the WGFP represented a potentially high-profile bilateral aid project. The project was revised and discussed at a workshop with NGOs in October 1990. The project proposal included macro-level zoning of the forests according to their broad management objectives, which was to be accompanied by a micro-planning process at the grassroots level, involving local communities. Though the project was much improved, NGOs were still concerned that the social-justice component needed to be strengthened; that the zoning process should be fully participatory; and that the project should oppose any resettlement of forest dwellers. They also argued that the role of NGOs in the project should be formally recognised.

Formal implementation of WGFP began in April 1992. The £24 million project, which was to run for an initial five-year pilot phase, was described by ODA as a 'process' project. This term denotes that 'the project emphasis is on processes rather than outcomes, on means rather than ends'. In other words, its approach was to be negotiable and evolutionary, in contrast to the traditional 'blueprint' project, with its emphasis on measurable in-puts. The project's aim was to assure the sustainability of the living standards of those people whose livelihoods currently derive in whole or in part from the forest. It was also 'to ensure that poor people, women, tribals, and other disadvantaged groups who are substantially dependent on the forests are not worse off, and preferably better off'.

The fundamental strategy was to enhance the management capacity of the KFD and to improve its responsiveness to conflicting demands from a range of users for access to the products of the forest. Monitoring was to be done, using milestones describing key stages which might change and develop as the project progressed. The basic tool for delivering sustainability was to be Joint Forest Planning and Management (JFPM). Joint Forest Management, JFM, is a form of common management in which responsibility for and benefits from the resource are shared with the government's forest department. JFM has been implemented in India for over 20 years and is widely promoted. ODA sought to build on JFM by developing the concept of Joint Forest Planning and Management. JFPM perceives the need for local participation in the planning processes and the explicit incorporation of development goals into the project's objectives.

Any change of access or use which would have an impact on local communities was to be arrived at through consultation. Information from local people was to be used to identify conservation zones, and they were to have a voice in the management of such areas. An initial rough zoning exercise was done by the KFD. But the project never reconciled the in-built tension between the bottom-up approach of micro-planning and the top-down methods of the KFD. Moreover, despite the rhetoric, JFPM was to be implemented in only 18 per cent of the forested area, and only 20 per cent of the project funds were allocated to participatory forest management.

From the beginning, ODA acknowledged that the project activities might have profound implications for certain social and income groups highly dependent on the forest, whose activities were believed to have a negative effect on forest regeneration: Gowlis (a caste of nomadic pastoralists), Siddis (descendants of slaves of African origin), Hallaki Vokkaliga (a sub-caste of cultivators), headloaders, and shifting cultivators. During the protracted negotiations, it was apparent that ODA shared Oxfam's concern about the project's wider social objectives. Unfortunately, this positive commitment to the poor became diluted in the final document. Considerable disagreement existed (and continues to exist) between ODA and KFD about the priority to be accorded to the project's objective of safeguarding the interests of disadvantaged groups. For its part, KFD reluctantly accepted JFPM as an inescapable adjunct to its now scaled-down afforestation project. KFD's lack of commitment to participation was reflected in the priority it gave to preliminary zoning based solely on technical considerations such as canopy cover and population distribution.

The first project circle

The northern-most Ghats district of Karnataka State, Uttara Kannada, was chosen to be the site of the first phase of the WGFP; the area was denominated by the project as the 'first circle'. The majority of Uttara Kannada's population are Hindus, but there are also sizeable minorities including Muslims, Christians, scheduled castes, and scheduled tribes. Seventy-seven per cent of the population are rural dwellers, the majority relying directly or indirectly upon agriculture; 23 per cent are urban dwellers, who are concerned mainly with trade. Forty-four per cent of villages had populations numbering fewer than 1,000. There are few village communities proper: the rural population lives in dispersed hamlets. Kannada remains the predominant language in the district, although Konkani, Marathi, and Arabic are also spoken.

Uttara Kannada (UK) is a forest-rich district: over 80 per cent of the total area is forested. Between 1960 and 1980 the quality of the forest sharply deteriorated. The rate of degradation was much higher in areas open to local use.[7] As researchers have noted, the integration of Uttara Kannada with the wider market economy has generally been at the expense of the local population, as local natural resources have been exploited, mined, or submerged to provide raw materials and power to fuel national industrial development. Not only has the impact on local employment and income-generation been marginal, but many locals have been dispossessed by new schemes. Local resentment grew, and the 1980s saw the emergence of an environmental protest movement called Appiko.[8] The struggle against the KFD focused upon the industrial use of forests, the monocultural plantations, the alienation of local people from the forests, and the neglect of local needs.

Forest access

Certain privileges exist in Uttara Kannada (the Kanara Privilege Rules) which give local people limited access to Reserve and Minor Forests and grant the comparatively well-off *arecanut*[9] farmers special access to protected forest land (*soppinabettas*). Kanara privileges allow the collection of dry leaves for manure, dead wood for fuel, and NTFP for household consumption only, as well as free grazing in the Minor Forest Area. KFD allows the exercise of these privileges in areas adjacent to officially recognised settlements and hamlets. These privileges can, however, be withdrawn by the KFD at any time. Poor people tend to live in newer settlements, where infringements of privilege rules are more easily identified and where privileges are more restricted and vulnerable to curtailment. Corruption and bribery are pervasive, and researchers have noted that knowledge of forest classifications and privileges granted is correlated to people's status and income.[10]

The failure of the privilege arrangements to operate satisfactorily was due partly to a lack of knowledge on the part of poor local people and to manipulation by contractors who gave them lower returns for the collection of NTFPs. The enforcement of regulations also proved ineffective, because the elite were simply able to buy additional (and usually illegal) benefits.

At the start of the Western Ghats Project, social groups in many villages in UK distrusted KFD officers, whom they perceived as corrupt bureaucrats exploiting local people. In order to obtain permission for felling or for the acquisition of timber, villagers had to apply in writing to the Range Officer. The mode of application (and the allegedly necessary bribe to speed the permission on its way) set this kind of contact beyond the reach of all but the wealthier farmers. There is evidence that wealthier groups have exploited more forest resources, even though it is poor peasants who are most dependent on forest resources for a proportion of their income. Clearly the roots of inequalities in access, use, and dependence on forest resources lie in the prevailing inequalities in society.

Joint management and Indian forest policy

JFPM represents a new approach to forest management, arising from the Indian National Forest Policy of 1988.

Until the mid 1980s forests were the domain of the Forest Departments; the management goal in the government controlled reserve forests was revenue generation; people living in and around forests — and deriving their livelihoods as gatherers — were viewed as part of the biotic interference from which forests were to be protected.[11]

The priority was to meet industrial and commercial demands for forest products and maximise State revenue. The Indian government's 1988 Forest Policy, which promoted the view that the forest resources should be managed for the environment and the promotion of livelihoods, radically transformed the old approach. Forests were to meet the basic needs of local communities, whose active participation would ensure the sustainable use of the resource. In particular the Forest Policy sought to change the adversarial relationship between the department and people to one of partnership. The government policy called for the protection of villagers' customary rights; prioritising the domestic requirements of local people for fuelwood, fodder, and non-timber forest produce and construction timber; enhancing the income and employment opportunities of local people by improving and increasing the production of NTFPs; and creating 'a massive people's movement, with the involvement of women', to achieve the policy's objectives.

Instructions were sent out from the Ministry of the Environment to all forest secretaries in all States, providing guidelines on how to involve village communities and voluntary agencies in the regeneration of degraded forests. Since then, 16 State governments have issued orders specifying their respective basis for working in partnership with local communities. However, in the opinion of the authors of an independent study of forestry in the Kanara Circle,

A major shortcoming of the Indian Government's guidelines is the restriction of villagers' participation in the regeneration of only degraded forests when the

forest policy itself, which the guidelines are intended to translate into practice, does not make any such distinction. This is emerging as a major impediment for the development of JFPM as a holistic alternative to traditional forest management.[12]

In November 1992 the Western Ghats Forestry Project was approved by the government of Karnataka. A condition of the project had been the issuing of a State government order facilitating JFPM. In 1993, the government of Karnataka duly issued an order establishing JFPM, but limited it to those forest areas which had a crown density of less than 25 per cent. Although ODA had stressed the importance of compatibility between the government order and the project's objectives, the Karnataka government's JFPM order was much more restrictive. In effect, by limiting JFPM to degraded forest areas, no participation was possible in decisions affecting the majority of the forest areas. (In December 1996, the government order was modified to allow JFPM to be implemented in areas of high forest density. But the Government Order specifies that VFCs can be formed only in areas where there are forest-dependent tribals. In the few cases where VFCs have been formed in Zone 3 areas, their legal status is uncertain. The Memorandum of Understanding with the Forest Department refers only to the entitlement of VFC members to collect NTFPs and to have access to grazing; but it does not specify a particular forest area.)

Village forest committees and micro-plans

Despite various misgivings about the scope of the government order and the interpretation of JFPM, NGOs in Karnataka have broadly welcomed the project, because for the first time JFPM has empowered local communities to manage areas of reserve forest with the Forest Department and to share in the benefits legally. The two essential elements of JFPM involve joint planning and joint management. Joint planning is a consultative process by which KFD, local people, and other forest-users jointly discuss the ecological and environmental conditions of a specific area of the forest, and the scope for it to meet one or more of their specific needs. The plan that emerges after consultations should as far as possible reflect all views; but the weight given to the different views will depend on the location of the area of forest in question and the types of vegetation it contains. Joint management of certain areas of forest will depend on their classification. Under joint management, the KFD and forest-users are supposed to divide responsibility for forest-management functions between them. They also agree on the division of the proceeds from the area under joint management

The core of JFPM is the village forest committee (VFC). It is the VFC which signs a legal contract, the Memorandum of Understanding, with KFD on how the joint management of the forest is to take place. Over the first five years of the project, some 216 VFCs were established in Uttara Kannada Circle.

The forests in the project area were to be divided into zones according to management objectives, which were to result from the joint planning process. Under JFPM, activities undertaken in specific areas of the forest would be in accordance with the specific characteristics of that zone. Five zones were initially identified; they ranged from the uninhabited, ecologically important areas[13] (zone 1) to the edge of forest reserves with forest-dwellers (zone 4). JFPM has a number of distinct stages:

1 preparation of profiles of the forest for the selection of priority areas for JFPM;
2 the identification of existing village groups, community institutions, and NGOs who might have a role in forming VFCs;
3 the preparation with VFC members of a micro-plan;
4 the signing of a memorandum of understanding (MoU) between KFD and the VFC.

The final stage concerns future monitoring and evaluating of the MoU. JFPM is presently limited to zone 4 areas where afforestation is undertaken and the benefits are shared in accordance with the government order. VFCs have largely been formed in villages which have degraded forests in their vicinity (until 1997 the government order restricted JFPM in degraded forest areas).

ODA had insisted on women being represented on the management committees of the Village Forest Committees. It had also been concerned that JFPM agreements should not conform to a uniform model. But, as a result of the highly restrictive JFPM government order, ODA did not adhere to its initial promise to NGOs that the project would ensure that all decisions on zoning would be participatory.

Oxfam's role in the Western Ghats Forestry Project

In 1993, Oxfam received a grant of £105,000 from ODA to undertake a three-year NGO/JFPM Support Project. The objective was to facilitate the involvement of local NGOs or other groups in the JFPM process and through them 'have a role in supporting the poorer user groups to participate effectively in JFPM'. The main purpose of Oxfam's project was to sustain and improve the status of poor people, and particularly women, tribals, the landless, and other disadvantaged groups, whose livelihoods depended on the Western Ghats forests.

Since the project began, Oxfam has sought to promote awareness of the purpose of JFPM; to enable local people, and especially the socially disadvantaged communities, to acquire the necessary skills to negotiate with the KFD; to facilitate the development of alternative sources of income generation; and to encourage the efficient production and marketing of NTFP assets by forest-users.

At the start of the project, the NGO presence in Uttara Kannada was relatively weak. Oxfam's field officer based in Sirsi, the main town in the project area, helped to identify and strengthen local NGOs and organised training programmes for NGO staff. Oxfam disseminated information about the WGFP and JFPM, and encouraged the formation of a district-level NGO co-ordination committee.

Oxfam's other concern was to promote income-generation programmes with NGOs. This included training in NTFP collection, processing, value addition, and marketing. In addition to promoting activities directly related to JFPM, Oxfam gave its support to some more traditional areas of work, including co-operatives, self-help groups, and thrift and credit groups as a means of reaching out to poorer sections of the communities.[14] By giving support to the formation of user groups, co-operatives, and youth clubs, Oxfam has attempted to explore various models of participation other than VFCs. According to Savio Carvalho, Oxfam's representative in Sirsi in the heart of the project area, 'if these groups are strengthened, then the overall objective of people taking control of their environment could gradually be achieved. In time, associations of people with common interests — after a lot of careful preparatory work — might begin to form the basis of autonomous VFCs.'

Oxfam allocated over 30 per cent of its grant to developing NTFP activities. 'NTFP' refers here to a wide variety of flora and fauna with commercial, edible, non-edible, or medicinal uses. Commercial NTFPs are collected and sold by the local population mainly to gain subsistence earnings; edible NTFPs are a major source of nutrition, collected by the local people for themselves or for their livestock. The more valuable NTFPs, such as bamboo, are either excluded from free access or are nationalised, with monopoly rights of collection and marketing vested with State agencies. Collection rights for such reserved NTFPs are auctioned or leased by the forest department to private contractors. The contractors employ local villagers through agents for the collection of NTFP, usually at exploitative rates.

Oxfam supported the work of a Siddi Co-operative Society in Manchikeri. The Siddis, descendants of African slaves, are resource-poor, forest-dependent communities. The greatest success of the Siddi co-operative has been to win a concession for the collection of *seegekai* (soapnut) in the local forest area for a two-year period between 1994 and 1996 (since renewed for a further two years). This represents a major step forward in terms of establishing the right of forest dwellers and collectors over NTFP. It has allowed the Siddis to work independently and to cut out the contractors and their agents. While in the first year the co-operative ran at a loss, owing to the depressed *seegekai* market, in the second year it made a profit of Rs. 100,000. Despite the fact that it will take some time to repay the loans, there is a real possibility of the co-operative's becoming self-sufficient in the near future.[15]

The work of local NGOs in Uttara Kannada

Certainly in the initial phases, the relations between KFD and local NGOs were strained. KFD was reluctant to share information with NGOs. There was also a tendency on the part of both KFD and ODA to relegate the issue of equity, gender, and poverty-awareness to the parallel NGO project, instead of ensuring that it was placed at the heart of the main Western Ghats Project. Even when departmental officers were well disposed to NGOs, they frequently expected them to undertake tasks for which KFD had no budget, such as disseminating fuel-efficient technologies, irrespective of the mandate and priorities of particular NGOs. KFD showed a marked tendency to limit NGO involvement to tasks which it considered to be a priority.[16]

NGOs have played a critical role in improving the design and implementation of the Western Ghats project. In areas where NGOs are active, the VFCs tend to have a greater sense of autonomy and ownership of the JFPM process. NGOs have been particularly successful in bringing women and other marginalised groups into the VFCs, and in helping to strengthen their voices in the decision-making process by first promoting smaller, more homogeneous self-help groups. They are acutely aware of the specific problems encountered by women, partly as a result of the gender-determined division of labour. In Uttara Kannada, women undertake a number of specific tasks both inside and outside the home, including food-preparation, house-cleaning, washing clothes and vessels, child care, family health care, fetching water, collecting fuelwood, and kitchen gardening. Women usually prepare a hot meal for their families twice a day. Household activities are often multiple, requiring simultaneous attention to other tasks, and felt by many women to be exhausting and never ending. Men in some cases help women in cutting trees for firewood or in child care, in the event of illness. The amount and intensity of women's productive activities depend on the agricultural season, the crops grown, and whether the land is irrigated. It also depends on class and age. Women undertake sowing, transplanting, and weeding. They cut paddy and collect freshly cut *arecanut* from trees. In wage labour, women, young girls, and boys receive the same wage rate, which is always lower than that of men, often for the same activity. There are peak periods during the agricultural season when women are under great pressure because they have to combine many activities within a fixed period of time, especially those who are wage labourers. When agricultural operations are undertaken on contract basis, women are under pressure to complete work in short periods. Productive work in the field is a single activity and therefore, even though it is hard and strenuous, it is considered less exhausting than the obligatory domestic tasks, which are entirely their responsibility. Generally men and women spend eight hours a day on agricultural work or wage labour, but women work an additional six hours in the homes. It is clear that women have an over-burdened work schedule, which leaves them little time for meetings. Nearly all Hindu communities in Uttara Kannada follow the system of patrilineal descent and inheritance, so that inheritance rights for land and livestock run in the male line. Women thus have no property rights, and in general, when part of a functioning family, do not own livestock or other assets.

Research has shown that when NGOs are present, the VFCs tend to meet more regularly, and there is greater transparency in the KFD's dealings with local people. The main constraint faced by NGOs is their limited spread and capacity. NGOs are able to work with only 51 of 212 VFCs which have been formed. Attempts are being made by NGOs to expand their reach through the creation of local VFC federations and to build up the villagers' own capacity to negotiate with the KFD. Efforts are also being expended in trying to ensure sustainability by forming VFC federations at *taluka* levels. This is seen firstly as a means of bringing VFC Presidents together to share views, but NGOs hope that in time they may be able to join forces to exert some pressure on the Forest

Department. The NGOs have also drawn up guidelines on the formation of VFCs which, in most cases, have not been implemented by the KFD.

NGO criticisms of the formation of VFCs

By 1993 18 VFCs had been formed. Planting was not envisaged to take place until micro-plans had been agreed — by the 1995 planting season. But KFD immediately started planting in 1993. KFD largely planted monocultures (rather than the promised multi-purpose, mixed-species plantations) that are incapable of meeting the various needs of local people. Although public meetings were held in each village to tell the local community about the project and to listen nominally to their suggestions for planting, nurseries had already been raised and pits dug before any consultation occurred. Planting was pre-determined by KFD. The overwhelming predominance of species like *acacia* and teak was, according to KFD, due to the fact that these were the only saplings available from their nurseries. NGOs were concerned that the status of other forest areas was not discussed with villagers, and that KFD appeared to disregard the needs of the landless poor for grazing areas. Although it had been understood that old plantations would come under VFC for benefit-sharing, no action was taken. During the first year of implementation, it became apparent that KFD was reluctant to include more valuable plantations of teak and cashew in the benefit-sharing scheme. Despite the rhetoric of the project document, NGOs could see little sign that the KFD was aware of the need to safeguard the livelihoods of vulnerable groups who depended on forest resources. Environmental NGOs were concerned about the almost total lack of interest on the part of the KFD in natural regeneration, which they argued would be more effective than plantations in providing local people with an adequate supply of their biomass needs.[17] Some NGOs came to the conclusion that the monocultural plantations, instead of enriching the area, were in fact leading to the destruction of the region's biodiversity. They criticised the KFD for its single-minded pursuit of improving tree cover at the expense of the WGFP's other objectives.

The VFC meetings were often held at short notice, at the convenience of the KFD, and they tended to be dominated by more powerful social groups and by men. NGOs were concerned about the influence of KFD over the VFC. Records were held by the forest officer, who was also responsible for taking the minutes of the VFC meetings.

NGOs warned KFD that rushing to form VFCs without due regard to social factors would be counter-productive. In 1993 NGOs observed that the majority of VFCs were formed in the one month preceding ODA's Annual Monitoring Mission, resulting in the creation of little more than paper committees. In the eyes of many villagers, who had very little understanding of JFPM or the project, the formation of a VFC represented a necessary administrative hurdle which had to be crossed in order to claim another government handout. In many areas, KFD was suspicious of NGOs and tried to discourage their involvement in the JFPM process.

It was sustained criticism by NGOs in Karnataka and Britain about the way the project was being implemented that led ODA to agree to fund an independent review of the Western Ghats Project.[18] In May 1995 a decision was taken in principle by ODA and KFD to extend the WGFP to a second circle, in Shimoga District. NGOs were concerned that, before the project was extended, lessons should be learned from the problems encountered with JFPM in the first circle. In 1996, after intensive lobbying by NGOs from Uttara Kannada about project implementation, ODA agreed to an independent review of the impact of the project in Uttara Kannada. The report of the distinguished Indian review team, which was published in May 1997, endorsed many of the NGOs' findings and criticisms.[19]

Summary of the findings of the independent review

Equity and exclusion in Village Forest Committees

The purpose of the Village Forest Committee is to provide a mechanism to ensure that the interests of all users of the forest are reflected in any eventual agreement reached with the KFD. This can happen only if each interest group is adequately represented, and if the VFC is able to facilitate negotiations between different sets of users, who may have competing needs and aspirations. Ideally the VFC needs to be able to assess the relative costs and benefits of various forms of forest management and arrive at a consensus in which the rights and interests of the most marginal and most forest-dependent users are protected. This can happen only in situations where all users are committed members of the VFC and feel confident in its ability to safeguard their respective interests.

The first problem is that 'revenue villages' have been selected as the appropriate unit for forming VFCs. Revenue-village boundaries have been administratively defined for the convenience of the government's revenue department, and they do not necessarily overlap with socially viable units of organisation. In Uttara Kannada there are few villages as such: the population lives in dispersed hamlets. No village exists in isolation from another. There are usually close dependency relationships linking villages together; these can be severely affected by any intervention that does not take this into account. There is a danger that, if JFPM assigns the forest to one particular village, it may deprive other users from adjacent villages of their customary access to crucial forest resources.

Even within villages, JFPM has the potential to cause harm. The independent review found that, in nearly half of the VFCs formed, many households were not members. In the majority of these cases, the non-members tended to be the poorest families in the village. Non-membership not only excludes the poorest from access to shares of income deriving from new plantations, but it also excludes them from information about JFPM and the decision-making process. On the other hand, those villagers who become members acquire the responsibility and authority to compel the non-members to conform to the VFC's decisions regarding areas of forest to be protected, and to respect new rules about access to and use of forest produce. This can have a dramatic impact on the rights of the poorest villagers to collect NTFPs on a day-to-day basis to meet their subsistence needs. The Karnataka government order fails to specify whether non-members continue to enjoy their customary rights and privileges in JFPM areas. Denial of such rights has serious implications and may become a future source of conflict.

Even in smaller VFCs which have full membership, but wide socio-economic disparities among the members, the leadership of the VFC is dominated by the landed elite. The review team found that, out of 17 VFCs visited, as many as seven were dominated by the wealthy elite. There is a very real danger that the wealthier members of the VFC may use JFPM as a means of gaining control over additional forest resources (thereby increasing their own political and economic power), while further reducing the access of marginalised groups who depend on forest resources to meet their basic needs.

Oxfam knows of one case where a VFC, primarily formed by poor women from landless households in the village of Banasgeri, was able to take over eight hectares belonging to their village, which had been encroached on by landowners from a neighbouring village. They are now cultivating the area under JFPM. This is one example, and possibly the only one to date, of a VFC successfully improving access of the poor to common-pool resources by obliging wealthier farmers to relinquish land they had illegally appropriated.

Negative impacts on the poor

Generally the review team found that JFPM failed to address the needs of the marginalised but highly resource-dependent communities. It feared that, unless this trend is checked, the project through 'a series of invisible and subtle processes of exclusion' will deprive the poor of their traditional access to forest resources.

In one village, Kamargaon, which is inhabited by a homogeneous community of resource-poor households, the entire village has been left worse off after forming a VFC. The KFD has used the JFPM process to stop the villagers from practising shifting cultivation, but this has left them without any alternative means of earning a living. The management plan has no provision for countering the negative impact of ending the practice of shifting cultivation. The VFC members instead must wait, many years, until the trees planted in the JFPM area, provided they survive, can be harvested. If all goes well, they will then acquire a share of the income.

The long lead-times associated with plantations impose an opportunity-cost on those previously utilising the area. These costs inevitably bear more heavily on vulnerable groups who require immediate benefits. The intermittent harvesting of monocrop plantations does not serve the needs of poorer groups for sources of forest produce that can be continuously harvested in small quantities.

Negative impact of JFPM on livestock

An estimated 20 to 30 per cent of landless households in Uttara Kannada maintain livestock as a supplementary source of income, or to provide products for domestic consumption. The planting of monocultures on grazing land has forced livestock owners to intrude into well-stocked forests in search of fodder. Milk is rarely affordable for landless households without livestock, so this milk production has an important nutritional function. Some of the rural poor, such as the Gowlis, gain their livelihoods mainly from their livestock. Most of the rural landless are wage labourers; work is seasonal and insecure. Gowlis used to make their living exclusively from milk sales, but this reliance has diminished in recent years as herd sizes have declined. The reasons include difficulties in providing enough fodder through grazing, even in settlements deep in the forest. The availability of grazing has suffered a serious decline in recent years as a result of three factors: the invasions of forest land by *Eupatorium*, a non-palatable weed which inhibits grass growth; the planting of trees on forest and grazing land near villages by the KFD; and the encroachment of forest and grazing land for agriculture. This increased the pressure on good forest areas. The decline in grazing has had a major impact on Gowli livelihoods, causing a direct reduction in their income through decreased sales of milk, manure, and animals. Many sharecroppers do not own land, and their ability to engage successfully in a tenancy is often dependent on ownership of livestock, particularly draught animals. For these people, livestock makes the difference between self-employment and dependence on wage labour, and is crucial to their livelihood system. Management of livestock by the landless places emphasis on flexibility and adaptation to the requirements of other income-generating activities, particularly wage labour. Because of the absence of land, reliance on free resources is greater, and free grazing, often in the forest, is maximised. A study of livestock ownership in Uttara Kannada, undertaken as part of the WGFP, revealed that 86 per cent of landless livestock keepers used the forest for grazing.[20] The decline in the availability of public grazing has hit the poor hardest, since they lack the private means to support their livestock. The review team was concerned that JFPM is already causing problems for poor livestock-owners as grazing areas are being taken over for plantations. The high proportion of species such as *acacia* and *casuarina* in the new plantations and the high-density planting practice preclude growth of grass for livestock between rows in plantations.

The poor have already reduced their livestock holdings as a result of the reduced grazing availability, and there is little room for adjustment of their livestock systems. Any further pressures are likely to lead to complete disposal of livestock and reduced livelihood options.

Obstacles to women's participation

In India about one third of all households are headed and solely supported by women. Such women-dependent households are disproportionately concentrated below the poverty line (GOI 1995) Yet, for the most part, in Uttara Kannada, despite ODA's good intentions, women remain outside the JFPM process; few women are even aware of the existence of VFCs in their villages. Only four out of 20 VFCs visited by the review team had any significant involvement of women in the running of the committee. The WGFP provides women in theory with two direct benefits. First, the free installation of astra-ole stoves, which reduce firewood consumption; but even in this the review team found that the women were treated as passive beneficiaries: only 40 per cent of the stoves work properly. The second benefit is waged employment in their villages on JFPM plantations.

Despite the fact that the Indian government, in order to curtail gender-determined discrimination and exploitation, has set a minimum wage of Rs. 47.25 for unskilled work, in most areas women are being paid by the KFD between Rs 20 and Rs 35.0, about half as much as is being paid to the men.

In India women are excluded from the public domain, and their interests have traditionally been regarded as belonging to the private realm.[21] To overcome this problem, ODA insisted that two places on the management committee of each VFC should be reserved for women. In practice, the women are often selected by the VFC chairman. In one village visited by the review team, two higher-caste women (Havik Brahmins) had been chosen: they had little contact with poor and landless women, other than when they hired them as casual labourers. Clearly in such cases the women management-committee members were not in any position to represent the interests of poorer women in the VFC.

In some villages, women attend the VFC meetings but sit quietly and serve tea and snacks. Some women fail to attend VFC meetings altogether, because there is no discussion of problems affecting them. In Hallibyle village, women complained that, whereas it used to take them less than an hour, they now spend two to three hours a day collecting a headload of leaves and twigs for cooking fuel. The scarcity of fodder and grazing areas has created similar difficulties for them. Only six of the 97 VFC members are women, so there was little objection when the VFC decided to sell off all the firewood harvested from their 30-hectare JFPM plantation, instead of using it to meet local consumption needs.

This pattern has been repeated in many villages in Uttara Kannada. Many women complained about the increased hardships they faced as a result of JFPM, but they had not felt able to raise their grievances at the VFC meetings. Women on the whole do not attend meetings, and feel powerless to influence decisions in the public domain. One NGO study described how one woman on the management committee was forbidden to attend the VFC meetings by her husband, who threatened to beat her if she went.[22] For poorer women the burden of labouring and harvesting virtually precludes their participation in meetings.

In some villages women told NGOs that the VFC meetings occurred only after the Memorandum of Understanding had been signed. These women had little idea how the management plan was to be implemented. Although they attended the signing of the MoU, they 'merely sat there like dolls'.[23]

It is clearly wrong to assume that the simple inclusion of two women on the management committee will take care of all women's interests.

Women will have to be selected in a more democratic fashion; they need to be aware of the need to hold regular consultations with other women before meetings in order to represent women's concerns, and then to report back after meetings on what decisions have been taken. All of this will require training and support.

Originally, the government order prescribed one representative per household, which had the effect of systematically excluding women from the VFCS and from active participation in JFPM. Although membership alone does not guarantee participation, it is clearly an important first step. In 1996 the Karnataka government amended the order to make 'spouses' automatically VFC members. But this still excludes a substantial number of male and female adults: marginalised individuals within households such as single women and men, widowed elders, second wives, and abandoned women, who may be some of the most resource-poor and forest-dependent individuals. Many women turn to headloading as a last resort after being abandoned by their husbands, or because their husbands spend their earnings on alcohol. There are also signs that the automatic membership of spouses is regarded as a kind of inferior membership (the membership fee of Rs 2 is waived) which does not entitle the person to an independent share in the VFC benefits. Women in many cases are reluctant to ask their husbands for their share of the benefits, in case they take offence and beat them.

NGOs have helped to create a few all-women VFCs, which according to the Independent Review have become 'vibrant and dynamic organisations', due no doubt in part to the additional struggle they have had to wage in order to establish women's right to participate in resource planning and management activities against established cultural norms.

The role of the KFD

NGOs and the review team have noted a marked improvement in the relationship between villagers and KFD officials since the start of the project. However, the government order places too much power and control of VFCs in the hands of the FD officer: he is the secretary of the VFC,[24] responsible for maintaining accounts, convening meetings, and preparing the joint management plans. Power to dissolve VFCs and to resolve potential conflicts and consider appeals is also vested in the FD officer. The KFD is also able to nominate or veto *ex officio* members, such as NGOs. The result is that the VFCs are accountable not so much to their members as to the KFD.

At present the way in which decisions are taken by the VFCs is not transparent. This is particularly obvious as regards expenditure and the basis on which wages are paid for JFPM-related work. In most VFCs, the majority of members are unclear about their rights and entitlements. Micro-planning and management plans tend to be drawn up by the FD officer, and focus on the plantation-centred, income-sharing model, to the detriment of alternatives more concerned with the satisfaction of livelihood or subsistence needs of local people, particularly the poorest.

Illusory benefits system

Under JFPM the VFC is responsible for protecting not only JFPM plantation areas but surrounding forests from encroachment, unregulated grazing, fire, illicit cutting, smuggling of forest produce, and the poaching of wild animals. In return, the only produce the members of the VFC are entitled to free of cost is grasses, leaves, and fuelwood, to all of which the villagers are already entitled under the Kanara Privilege Rules.

The government order states that the requirements of local villagers should have first call on minor forest produce, fruits, timber and the final harvest from plantations. Any surplus can then be disposed of by the VFC through public auction. Since it was not thought possible to determine the precise needs of the villagers, the government order then specified that '50 per cent of the minor forest produce, fruits, timber and final harvest shall, until further orders, be made available for local sale through VFCs to meet the needs of local villagers at the rates to be fixed by the KFD'. The surplus 50 per cent will be sold through public auction (p.84 clause 17 iii).

This means that the KFD and the VFC are entitled to 50 per cent each of the net income obtained through the sale of forest produce. But the VFC's share is then to be divided into two parts, half of which is to go to a village forest-development fund and the remaining 25 per cent to be distributed equally among VFC members. As the independent review observes, 'This apparently simple formula appears attractive ... creating the impression that villagers will start getting shares of income from forest produce. However, if the villagers first buy 50 per cent of the produce at local rates, then their 25 per cent share of the net income will actually consist of the money that they themselves have already paid initially when buying the produce for their own needs.' Rather than villagers receiving shares of income from their JFPM plantations, they will in effect be getting their own money back. In effect, the revenue-sharing formula is an extremely complicated savings scheme, creating the illusion that villagers are earning new income. In other words, 'the disposal and sharing provision offers the villagers only two choices — either get some of the produce free through the complex system of first paying for it, or get some money instead of the produce'. No other State JFPM order obliges the villagers to buy their share of the produce.

This complex system in some cases has had the effect of the poor subsidising the better-off. In Honnebail village, instead of keeping the firewood from the main harvest to provide women greater relief from the daily chore of collecting leaves and twigs, the men decided to sell off all the firewood to get the money. So the men received Rs 548 each, in part the fruits of women's having worked longer hours on a regular basis for several years. JFPM should give the actual resource-users the first right to decide what they want to do with the produce generated by their indirect labour.

PRA — an empty ritual

Participatory rural appraisal, PRA, is a set of approaches and methods which has been increasingly adopted in the 1990s by development staff in both NGOs and official donor agencies. PRA is supposed to enable local people to share, enhance, and analyse their knowledge of life and conditions. It is designed to generate insights which can shape development interventions. PRA is seen as a means of enabling local people to monitor and evaluate these interventions. Used particularly in natural-resource management projects, it presents an alternative to traditional development techniques such as questionnaire surveys, and seeks to transform local people from passive beneficiaries into active participants. For its exponents, PRA is a corrective to the past domination by external experts of the development process. But PRA has been a victim of its own success: its rapid proliferation has led to bad practice. 'The label has spread without the substance.'[25]

The joint forest-management plan has three stages: a micro-plan, a management plan, and a Memorandum of Understanding signed by both KFD and the VFC. The micro-plan is supposed to be a village map, giving a profile of the village and providing socio-economic and resource data. The Management Plan is supposed to contain objectives arising out of the micro-plan. It includes a zonation map and sets out a five-year action plan, detailing issues to do with conservation, access, and protection. The MoU lists benefits and responsibilities of the VFC. The ODA project involved an ambitious training programme for KFD officers in Participatory Rural Appraisal techniques to enable them to work with villagers in drawing up social maps and conduct needs-assessments. However, the review team, while recognising that the KFD officers devoted a lot of time and effort to preparing these plans, found a number of problems with them. Despite the use of PRA techniques, essentially it is the KFD officers who prepare the plans. The villagers' participation is limited to providing the officers with information. The PRA is normally completed in a day, often in only half a day. But this very compressed time-scale makes the information gathered suspect and unreliable. In practice, not only are the plans primarily being prepared by KFD officers on their own, but also the process fails to ensure the participation of all groups of forest-users within the community. There is evidence to suggest that PRA has become a mechanical exercise which has little input into the final management plan. In Uttara Kannada, NGOs complained that, during the first stage of the project, in many villages PRA and the management plans were undertaken only *after* JFPM areas had been selected and planted by the KFD, with little or no involvement of local people. Simply adding up individual household requirements and planning to meet them in aggregate terms not only overlooks the differential access of different members to what is proposed to be generated, but also neglects to consider when and how biomass is needed. Daily firewood requirements cannot be satisfied by plantation harvests once every few years. Failure to incorporate an analysis of gender-determined roles related to forest use among different categories of forest-users means that the needs of poorer female forest-users have not been adequately addressed.

The training in PRA and micro-planning is not equipping KFD staff adequately to prepare more meaningful management plans. In good PRA practice, participatory behaviour and attitudes matter more than methods. Robert Chambers, one of the leading exponents of PRA, warns that it can be done badly. 'PRA has been known at first to omit people, such as minority groups, migrants, outcastes, those who live on the fringes or outside villages'.[26] But many would question whether, in the WGFP, PRA techniques have been used at all. *Rapid* rural appraisal (RRA) would appear to be a more accurate description of KFD's approach, and its version of this methodology is far from participatory. RRA has tended to involve the use of secondary sources and observation. It relies on semi-structured interviews and focus groups. In RRA those in a position of authority never lose control of the process. In PRA, however, the idea is to reverse roles — making local people the experts.

They then undertake analysis, and social and resource mapping, they prepare plans and budgets, carry out activities related to the project, and then take responsibility for monitoring and evaluation. RRA is predominantly a method of extracting data, whereas PRA aspires to be a process of empowerment.

Conclusion and recommendations

In the WGFP, both ODA and the KFD accepted the crucial importance of involving the poor and women in natural-resource management, since failure to meet their needs might result in the violation of community agreements out of desperation. Unlike the World Bank's PLANAFLORO project in Brazil, there has also been from the outset a conscious attempt to design a mechanism for participation that could promote the emergence of viable autonomous local institutions. The Karnataka project was to fund a number of socio-economic studies. In effect this meant that the project proceeded before the findings of these studies were available, and, although studies spelled out the danger of adverse impacts on poor, forest-dependent people, no contingency funds were set aside to compensate them for the loss of crucial resources. At the start of the forest-zoning programme, neither ODA nor the KFD had a clear understanding of the potential risks to the poor or vulnerable groups. In the absence of adequate social assessment, the project failed to incorporate safeguards which could mitigate any negative impacts that JFPM might have on vulnerable groups during implementation. Nor did the project specify how the belatedly available research findings were to be incorporated into project activities. While the project has encountered a number of problems, ODA has shown itself prepared to work with KFD, the NGOs, and local communities to improve performance. The final result of the project will largely depend on the willingness of the different actors to apply the lessons learned from the difficulties that have been encountered during the first phase of the project.

Change the emphasis on targets

The ODA saw the WGFP as a pilot programme which would guide the implementation of JFPM throughout Karnataka. But the Karnataka government order applied JFPM to the entire State, and not simply to the project area. This not only weakened the ODA's influence over the legal framework for JFPM, but also created an anomalous situation whereby the project in Uttara Kannada circle was implementing the same official

State policy, but with many more resources and staffing than were available elsewhere. ODA envisaged a much slower pace of growth for VFCs, but this was incompatible with the government of Karnataka's target of 300 VFCs to be created in the financial year of 1993/94 — the first year of the project. One of the most serious problems identified by the independent review team was the rigid target-oriented approach which is followed in forestry for afforestation programmes. Too great an emphasis on high levels of planting has crowded out other management options, such as natural regeneration, which is far cheaper and more cost-effective.[27] Fodder production has not been given sufficient priority. And there is no system for the evaluation of these interventions, particularly in terms of their social impact. As a result, KFD's efforts to improve the long-term viability of projects and to secure people's co-operation are neither monitored nor insisted upon. The bulk of project funds get earmarked for planting schemes which have a low rate of survival. The primary monitoring activities of KFD focus largely on fiscal accountability at the expense of other aspects of their work. Failures are not reported and analysed, and the recommendations from workshops are not followed up. Despite ODA's concern that the formation of a VFC should not be a mechanical process but a response to local people's desire to participate (resulting from the project's success in mobilising and educating forest-dependent communities in Uttara Kannada), the speed of implementation has outstripped the pace of training. The quantitative targets set by KFD both for the formation of VFCs and plantations has undermined the 'process' approach.[28]

Support for 'user' nurseries

At present KFD controls nurseries and provides VFCs with saplings that 'are available' — usually acacia or teak. Nurseries and other potential sources of saplings need to recognise people's preferences, and the project should ensure that a variety of saplings is available. Oxfam believes that there is a strong case for the project to support the development of user nurseries.

A more flexible approach: site-specific planning

Attempts by ODA to address the problems, particularly with the extension of the WGFP to another district, Shimoga, rely on the application of what is termed 'site-specific planning'. This entails having a decentralised budgeting system to give field staff a greater say in what work is most appropriate for a particular area of forest. It also signifies a shift away from the artificial construction of the VFC. It is evident that forest areas in Uttara Kannada utilised by villagers are not clearly bounded or mutually exclusive. It is almost impossible to define a specific forest area as the exclusive resource-base for a particular and co-residential set of people. Different users within the village often have an interest in different products, or different interests in the same product. The shift to site-specific planning is to encourage KFD to assess the range of interest groups and users as an essential preliminary to any form of planning. It should help to move the system of management away from prescriptive management models towards a more flexible approach. The KFD is to adhere to the principle that as far as possible it is seeking to ensure that the multiple objectives of a range of interest groups are met. The stakeholders will no longer be identified as people living within the boundaries of a 'revenue village', but will include all those who use the forest and derive benefit from it. However, some environmentalists believe that site-specific planning is too reliant on technical aspects of computer-ised management tools (like the Range Management Information System), and they point out that this has already had the effect of alienating local people from forest management. There is the additional problem that the dominant planning tool of the Forest Department — the working plans (recently bolstered by a Supreme Court ruling insisting on their use) — is not at present compatible with site-specific planning.

Reintegrate JFPM staff into KFD

The project has abandoned the idea of having a separate cadre of specially selected and trained foresters to undertake JFPM. This has not worked well: other staff have not been willing to co-operate with JFPM, and there is ambiguity about their responsibilities. JFPM staff feel marginalised and out of the mainstream of KFD. For many, being assigned to JFPM work signified a demotion. A lot of the training has been wasted, as there has been a high turnover of staff. KFD have felt that the numerous work-shops and meetings promoted by the WGFP have taken up too much time and removed officers from their primary tasks of forest protection. KFD officers have complained that workshops have been held too often and there has not been sufficient time to allow them to absorb new ideas. Their view is that there are too many consultants trying to accomplish too many things. Many changes have been introduced into the project without allowing officers sufficient time to adjust.

Transform VFCs

A crucial indicator of how well VFCs perform as people's organisations will be the extent to which they are able to address the concerns of livelihood-generation and sustainable management. JFPM so far has not been able to create VFCs which are robust, self-governing, and autonomous, capable of managing forest resources in a responsible and equitable manner. VFCs are too dependent on KFD: their operating systems, rules, and norms are underdeveloped; members participate in meetings only after considerable cajoling; often, members do not know why they are members, and even VFC management committees are not clear about the benefits and obligations of these committees. According to the Independent Review, if JFPM is to succeed in its aim to alter the relationship of people to the forests, it has to provide the community with a bundle of rights to set against a range of obligations. For this new relationship to be meaningful, a number of conditions have to be met:

- communities must have a full understanding of the agreement with the Forest Department;

- the agreement must be worthwhile;

- the community must be able to devise easy and practical ways of ensuring that each member adheres to it;

- the community must be able to impose graduated sanctions in case of non-compliance with the agreement;

- and the whole community needs to be organised into a self-governing entity which is empowered and has a large space for decision-making.

In 1997 the government of Karnataka amended the State Forest Law to allow for the constitution of legally recognised Village Forest Committees 'for the purpose of Joint Forest Planning and Management'. Unfortunately the scope of the act is limited to the small number of village forest lands and will apply to very few of the existing Village Forest Committees in the Western Ghats. The government order in fact is little more than a token amendment, falling far short of what is required to make Joint Forest Planning and Management effective.

A broader membership base

In order to enable VFCs to become institutions which draw on all forest users, irrespective of their marital or household status, the government

JFPM order should be urgently amended to make all adult members of the social units comprising the VFCs eligible for independent membership. Further, the sharing of benefits should be on the basis of individual membership, and not on the basis of households. Management plans have to provide viable alternatives for all those currently dependent on JFPM areas which are closed to grazing and extraction. The resource-poor cannot wait for several years without any means of satisfying their daily consumption needs. The micro-planning process needs to incorporate an analysis of the differing, often conflicting, needs and priorities of different socio-economic groups of women and men among the VFC membership. Priority should be given to meeting the needs of the most resource-poor. An essential component of PRA should be an analysis of gender roles related to forest use among different categories of forest users. In the longer term, JFPM should aim not only to address effectively the needs of poorer female forest-users but also to reduce gender-related differences in their burden of work and access to resources.

Improving women's participation

As women are the most significant if not the largest single group of forest users, their absence from the VFC decision-making process has often resulted in their priorities remaining unheard, and the impact of increased labour and time required for daily chores such as firewood gathering and hand-harvesting of grass is unknown. If the needs and priorities of primary forest-users continue to be ignored under JFPM, then groups may revert to unsustainable exploitation. In Uttara Kannada at present, unsustainable resource exploitation by women and other marginalised groups simply gets transferred to other parts of the forest — defeating the whole purpose of JFPM. In less-forested areas of Karnataka this option will not be available.

NGOs are uncertain whether these adjustments will be enough to ensure that JFPM safeguards the interests of the poorest and most disadvantaged sections of the communities. They point out that the KFD's interpretation of key project policies has been conservative and its approach to JFPM has been bureaucratic, despite the adoption of the language of community management. The formation of VFCs has been mechanical and planting-led, with 'participation' consisting of heavy-handed persuasion of local users to support traditional departmental objectives. The measure of the ability of ODA's process approach to facilitate a change of direction in the attitudes and management style of

KFD will be tested in the second circle. As the project proceeds in the more socially diverse and complex Shimoga district, which has a much more significant degree of forest degradation, different approaches to JFPM will be more keenly felt. It remains to be seen whether KFD's conversion to 'community management' is more than an empty gesture, a calculated step taken to acquire donor funding for the afforestation project it originally envisaged, or whether it marks a fundamental change of direction of lasting significance.

A lot is at stake. For more than a century, State forest departments in India have wielded enormous power and authority, but have not been accountable to forest-dependent villagers. In the long run, JFPM partnerships will be durable and successful only if they are rooted in mutual acceptance of clearly defined rights and responsibilities by both the Forest Department and community institutions. At present there is a danger that KFD's conventional, top–down planning and management tradition may simply be extended to an equally centralised and inflexible prescription of rules and regulations for the creation, structure, and functioning of community organisations which the department expects to participate in JFPM. Such an approach, which assumes that people's participation and the creation of village institutions can be achieved through executive *fiat*, is doomed to fail.

4 Global benefits, local costs: expulsion from the Kibale Forest

In the mid-1980s, world-wide concern about the rapid depletion and degradation of natural resources and its impact on the global environment generated a host of international responses: internationally funded national environmental action plans, conservation strategies and projects. The European Commission (EC), in common with other donors, changed the overall emphasis of its projects away from forest-based industrial development towards the promotion of conservation.[1] Between 1987 and 1991 under Lomé III (the Development Co-operation Treaty between the European Community and African, Caribbean, and Pacific countries) 22 African countries received funding for 41 environmental projects, mainly for the protection of tropical forest ecosystems. But, as the case-study in this chapter will show, the EC has failed adequately to address the needs and rights of local populations.[2] Many environmental projects established before 1992 were designed without any form of consultation with potential beneficiaries, and, as a review of EU evaluation reports indicates, 'consultation of the key players in the political and social context' of the projects did not frequently occur. After surveying a sample of more than 80 projects, the review concluded that 'the involvement of beneficiaries or users in EC-assisted interventions is consistently weakly represented'.[3] The EC's environmental efforts — at least in East Africa — appear to have been based on the assumption that conservation could best be achieved by removing local people from protected areas.

Despite the fact that involuntary resettlement has been one of the most carefully studied problems associated with development, the new generation of Community-funded environmental projects and programmes did not draw on the lessons from traditional infrastructure projects.

This chapter looks at the devastating consequences that can occur when donors make no attempt either to enable local people to participate in natural-resource management or to safeguard their rights and livelihoods. The first section examines the importance of adherence to aid guidelines such as those concerning Involuntary Resettlement. The next section describes what happened under the EC-funded Natural Forest Management and Conservation Project in Uganda and sets this in the context of the then existing macro-economic and conservation policies of the government of Uganda. It examines deficiencies in the approach of the donors, and particularly the EC, to aid-management. The final section looks at both the short-term and long-term consequences of the displacement from the Kibale Forest, the response of the EC, and the political and economic unsustainability of this model, which seeks to provide global benefits while leaving the costs to be borne by local, poor people.

Involuntary resettlement

Involuntary resettlement is the best-understood and most widely publicised negative consequence of development. It has been 'indelibly written into the evolution of industrial as well as developing countries'.[4] Involuntary displacement continues to occur in all countries for many different reasons, although it has been mostly associated with the construction of large dams and highways. In the developing world, large dam-construction projects (some 3,000 of which are initiated each year) are estimated to be leading to the displacement of four million people. Urban development and transport projects account for the displacement of a further six million people. That means that each year as many as ten million people are uprooted and impoverished by development projects. According to the World Bank, over the past decade 80–90 million people have been resettled as a result of infrastructure projects.

The World Bank acknowledges that the potential for violating individual and group rights under domestic and international law makes compulsory resettlement unlike any other project activity. When resettlement is carried out in a lawful manner that fully respects the rights of resettlers and host communities, opposition to projects is reduced. Carrying out resettlement in a manner that respects the rights of affected persons is not just an issue of compliance with the law: it also constitutes sound development practice. Based on its experience of the lessons it learned from large-scale development projects in the 1970s, in 1980 the World Bank adopted a resettlement policy. Over the years the policy was strengthened and incorporated the findings of social science research on resettlement.[5] By issuing resettlement-policy guidelines and procedures, the Bank became the first multilateral institution to enact a policy framework for displacement and to provide a benchmark for standards on resettlement, which were slowly incorporated into the policies of other donors.[6]

The key elements of the Bank's resettlement policy are as follows.

- Involuntary displacement should be avoided or minimised whenever possible, because of its disruptive and impoverishing effects.

- Where displacement is unavoidable, the objective of Bank policy is to assist displaced persons in their efforts to improve, or at least restore, former living standards and earning capacity. The means to achieve this objective consists of the preparation and execution of resettlement plans, which should be integral parts of project designs.

- Displaced persons should be (a) compensated for their losses at replacement cost, (b) given opportunities to share in project benefits, and (c) assisted in the transfer and in the transition period at the relocation site.

- Resettlers and the 'hosts' (the community already living in the vicinity of the relocation site) should participate in planning the resettlement.

While it may not always be possible for donors, despite their best efforts, to guarantee a completely successful outcome, it is invariably the case that where preparation and monitoring are slack, the potential for causing damage is hugely increased. The problems that have arisen in the context of the Western Ghats Forestry Project (examined in the previous chapter) are dwarfed in comparison with the scale and intensity of suffering which a poorly conceived and badly implemented project can have on the lives of poor communities.

Natural Forest Management and Conservation Project, Uganda

Between 1990 and 1993, more than 130,000 people were evicted — some forcibly — from forest areas in Uganda, as part of the European Commission's Natural Forest Management and Conservation Project. The project was designed to assist the Ugandan Forest Department to clear the forests of encroachers. The most violent evictions occurred in

A map of Uganda, showing Kibale

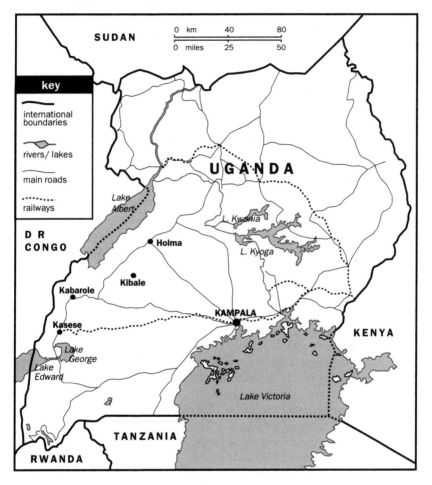

April 1992, when some 35,000 people were evicted from the Kibale Forest Reserve and Game Corridor. There were reports of serious violations of human rights during the evictions, resulting in a number of deaths. No provision had been made to resettle the families, and those evicted were left destitute, begging along the roads with no food or shelter. There was a public outcry in the country, and President Museveni directly intervened, promising those who had been evicted the chance to resettle in another part of the country.

After the evictions, thousands of displaced people had to resort to squatting in shopping centres or working as farm labourers in exchange for space for their temporary shelters. Some worked as sharecroppers or as cheap labour for local landowners. Those who attempted to return to their plots of land and collect food from their stores were allegedly beaten by guards. Those who moved to the neighbouring district of Kasese found themselves in an even more desperate state: with water and food in scarce supply, they could only find some temporary base along the railway line in appalling conditions. They even faced the ultimate indignity of having nowhere to bury their dead. There is no accurate record of how many people died, but the old, the young, and vulnerable people like pregnant women succumbed in these first few terrible months. These conditions prevailed until September 1992, when finally efforts were made by the government to resettle them in Bugangaizi, in the District of Kibaale. (Kibaale District, which includes the sub-county of Bugangaizi in which those displaced were resettled, is distinct from the Kibale Forest and Game Corridor where the evictions occured — despite the close similarity of the names.)

The Natural Forest Management and Conservation Project formed part of a major Forestry Rehabilitation Project in Uganda, worth $38 million and co-ordinated by the World Bank. The Forestry Rehabilitation Project was identified and appraised by the World Bank in 1987 and broken down into six separate components, which were taken up by various donors, including the European Commission. In January 1988 the EC agreed to finance the Natural Forest Management and Rehabilitation component. During the five-year period of the project, total disbursements from the European Development Fund (EDF) amounted to 11 million ecus.

The principal objectives of the EC Project were the demarcation of forest boundaries; the establishment of nurseries and replanting of 26,000 hectares of encroached or degraded forest; improving forest patrolling, supervising charcoal-production, logging-management, and revenue-collection; the establishment of management plans; and increasing the conservation area to 50 per cent of the total of 1,400,000 hectares of natural forest.

An evaluation of the EC's project noted that, although the Ugandan Forest Department and other government institutions were involved in the preparation, either the EC nor the World Bank consulted or informed forest dwellers, those living adjacent to the forest, or those using forest products, either about the project or about its implications. Although social issues were identified in the design stage, they became subordinated to a forestry-oriented approach aimed at controlling the Forest Reserves. As a result the project did not reflect the priorities of the people living in and around the forests. Local people were not considered as participants, stakeholders, or beneficiaries, and the subsequent implementation of the project did not take account of their immediate needs and interests.[7]

Environmental degradation in Uganda

Violence and misfortune had plagued Uganda from the mid-1960s for almost two decades. Between Uganda's independence in 1962 and 1986, national leadership changed seven times. Hundreds of thousands of Ugandans died or 'disappeared' in armed conflicts between 1971 and 1986. Eventually, after five years of guerrilla war, the National Resistance Movement (NRM) gained enough strength to achieve a victory and assume the national leadership in January 1986. Since then, the internal security situation has much improved, and Uganda is one of the most stable countries in the region. In September 1995 a new Constitution was approved and in the following year this was consolidated when elections for the Presidency and Parliament took place.

Protecting forest reserves was a key element in the efforts of the government of Uganda to address the problem of environmental degradation which had been exacerbated during the twenty-year break-down in law and order. The lack of controls and of adequate enforcement measures had contributed to the encroachment of over 70 per cent of Uganda's gazetted forests. In the late 1980s, the government, spurred on by the availability of overseas development assistance for environmental projects, resolved that all people who had encroached on any part of gazetted National Parks, Forests, and Game Reserves should be evicted.

By the mid-1980s the country had experienced fifteen years of political crisis and civil turmoil, leading to a social and economic collapse in which real GDP fell by 20 per cent and many skilled people were either killed or left the country. The physical infrastructure had been badly damaged and economic production was stagnant. The new government taking control in January 1986 inherited a demoralised civil service which was poorly paid and widely seen as corrupt. Government departments could barely function, and the rate of inflation reached 200 per cent. It was against this background that the government embarked on a process of economic recovery and the reintroduction of the rule of law. A structural adjustment programme was agreed in 1987 and, following the lead of the World Bank and the IMF, donors sought to underpin the government's programme of political stability and economic recovery. The EDF National Indicative Programme for Uganda, agreed in January 1987, gave priority to rehabilitation and reconstruction of the economic and social infrastructure. The forest sector had sound development potential, and donors believed that it could make an important contribution to the national economy through the production of timber and fuel-wood. In the view of consultants working for the World Bank and the EC, this rehabilitation could not take place before the removal of those who had encroached on the gazetted forest estate. This was seen as part of the process of restoring the rule of law.[8]

Oxfam's concern is focused on the absence of any coherent plan which would have minimised the adverse impact on affected families; and on the failure of the donor agencies responsible for drawing up and implementing environmental projects to recognise this problem, and act in accordance with good aid practice. The donors also conspicuously failed to take robust action to remedy problems, once the evictions began and the scale of suffering became apparent.

Increasingly it has come to be acknowledged in different parts of Africa that conservation strategies to protect natural resources are much more likely to succeed if local people are involved. There are abundant examples of participatory approaches to natural-resource management, such as the Campfire Programme in Zimbabwe. It is regrettable that the World Bank and the EC failed in Uganda to promote a more progressive and enlightened approach in the Kibale Forest project. Within the government of Uganda, from 1986, there was a move towards participation by local people in local government through the system of Resistance Councils, intended to encourage people to plan development projects. However, the EC Natural Forest Management and Conservation Project did not attempt to incorporate this in its approach to dealing with encroachment. Nor did the project specify local community groups as major stakeholders, either as participants or beneficiaries. Encroachment was narrowly seen to be an issue of law and order.[9]

Ugandan Conservation Policy

Under Ugandan law, a national park is defined as an area that has been accorded the highest conservation status, protecting natural and scenic areas of natural and scientific use. In Uganda's national parks, prohibited activities include settlement and other forms of land use.

Various pieces of legislation specify how public land is to be governed and used. Those who contravene the law may be punished, not only through imprisonment and fines but also through the forfeit of property and developments on the illegally acquired land. Apart from the application of criminal sanctions, the State can re-establish its rights to the land only by evicting the illegal occupants. The prohibition of encroachers on gazetted land — Forest Reserves, Game Reserves, Game Corridors, and National Parks — is covered by the Forest Act and the Game (Preservation and Control)Act.

Since the late 1980s, the Forest Department has carried out evictions in five national parks.[10] Detailed data on the total number of people evicted are scarce; but, according to the Forest Department, the figure is between 30,000 and 40,000, excluding a further 64,000 people removed from forest reserves. A government report on resettlement noted that there has been an absence of policy guidelines, and admitted that 'valuation and compensation may have been carried out in an arbitrary fashion'.[11]

Integrated conservation and development projects

In the 1980s the Ugandan government embarked on a number of conservation projects known as Integrated Conservation and Development Projects — ICDPs. The concept behind ICDPs was to integrate development and conservation strategies, but the objective of most ICDPs has been to improve the protection and preservation of important ecosystems. Subsequent evaluations have confirmed that these projects tended to concentrate on conservation imperatives to the exclusion of all other concerns. The Mount Elgon ICDP, for example, which was financed by the Norwegian Government and executed by International Union for the Conservation of Nature and Natural Resources (IUCN), was evaluated in 1993. The report concluded that 'the original strategy was too biased towards protection, [and that] the rural development programme was not adequately linked to forest use and issues of sustainable forest resource management'. Thousands of people were evicted from Mount Elgon between 1988 and 1993 by the Forest Department, which, according to the report, generated considerable resentment and left unresolved conflicts as a result.[12] One of the most serious legacies of this approach has been the alienation of local communities from conservation efforts.

Deficiencies in the donors' approach

There was increasing international pressure during the 1980s to upgrade the conservation status of some of Uganda's forest reserves. In 1982 IUCN identified six priority forest areas, which became the focus of the EC's project. A National Environmental Action Plan was drawn up which attempted to provide an environmental policy framework and produce a balance between production and conservation. But the EC project did not reflect the growing support for community participation in conservation efforts, nor the importance of integrating conservation and rural development needs. Instead, the project promoted a traditional 'fortress' approach to forest management which was largely discredited by the time the project was being implemented. It is now widely recognised that it is impossible to maintain forest control solely by a policy of excluding people, without the balance introduced by forms of participatory management.[13]

Although the government of Uganda had not developed its own guidelines on resettlement, it was incumbent upon the donor agencies' staff to respect and implement existing aid guidelines. EC officials have pointed in mitigation to their limited staff capacity and ability to monitor projects as they would wish. But the fact remains that in Uganda best practice, official guidelines, and operational directives were consistently ignored or flouted. Failings by local World Bank and EC staff were then overlooked by their managers in headquarters.

The World Bank failed in its duty as the agency responsible for the identification, preparation, and appraisal of the project to draw attention to the inevitability of involuntary resettlement in the forest-conservation component; and it failed to draw up resettlement plans and incorporate these into the project documents. The 1987 World Bank Staff Appraisal Report (SAR) should have followed the operational directive on involuntary resettlement then in place[14] by indicating the need for a properly costed resettlement plan for displaced people and ensuring that the cost and plan were integrated into the final project document. The SAR side-stepped the existence of long-term encroachers in the forest reserves and referred merely to the need 'to increase the area of natural forest identified as natural reserves from 5 per cent to 20 per cent during the project period'. In one section concerning demarcation of forest boundaries, the SAR refers to the fact that 'there has been serious encroachment by agriculturalists'.

The World Bank's initial failure to highlight the implications of displacement for the project had particularly serious consequences. The

EC, even more than most other donors, relies heavily on the quality of the preparatory work of the World Bank, and does not normally undertake its own project-appraisal or conduct additional environmental impact assessments when it takes over a Bank-prepared component. The EC has generally lagged behind other donor agencies in developing policy guidelines and procedures. Before 1993 it had not even drawn up a manual on how to conduct Environmental Impact Assessments (the use of which became mandatory only in 1996). Although Lomé III for the first time explicitly refers to gender issues, there is no evidence that staff ever undertook any analysis of the likely impact of projects on women. Indeed, most evaluations confirm the virtual absence of gender-related considerations, and the general lack of gender-disaggregated data in most EC projects of the period. Evaluation reports indicate that it is not only gender issues that have been neglected in financing proposals. It is true to say that the Commission has undertaken very limited analysis of the socio-economic and cultural context of its projects in general.[15] The majority of environmental projects started before 1992 were designed without any form of consultation. A substantial proportion of environmental projects still fail to take the views of local communities into account during preparation. This is problematic, for it means that projects do not address social issues the solutions to which often require a participatory approach.

It is not surprising that the EC did not conduct its own check on the likely impact on encroachers of enforcing forest boundaries. Yet, according to the EC's Chief Technical Adviser, both EC and World Bank staff were aware of the implications:

For political reasons, dealing with the encroachment issue was not shown as an objective in the World Bank's Staff Appraisal Report or in the EC's Financing Agreement (1988), although it was obvious to those on the missions involved that nothing would be achieved without the eviction of squatters and a firm control of encroachments.[16]

At almost no stage in the implementation of the project did senior staff members of either the World Bank or EC question the compatibility of the Ugandan government's evictions policy with existing World Bank guidelines or with the underlying principles of European aid. The issue appears never to have been raised at any of the donors' co-ordination meetings. In February 1990, for example, the Bank's supervision mission, disregarding World Bank policy, commented that the EC programme 'has made significant achievements in removing encroachers from the high forest...'.

Although when it first approved the project the EC had no formal guidelines on involuntary resettlement, by 1992 — the time of the Kibale evictions — the EC had adopted and was bound by OECD Guidelines on Involuntary Displacement and Resettlement (OECD/GD 201).[17] But capacity in the EC's Delegation and concerted action to ensure that they were acted on in a timely way were lacking.

Most Ugandans are cultivators: agriculture accounts for over 60 per cent of the GDP, about 68 per cent of export earnings, and over 40 per cent of government revenue. Farming is labour-intensive, with women providing 60–80 per cent of the labour for cash crops sold in local markets and food crops for home consumption. The non-monetary economy is also very significant, constituting 44 per cent of the GDP (almost all in agriculture). According to a recent UNICEF-sponsored report, 'It is the resilience of subsistence agriculture which has sustained most Ugandans for many years. Land ownership and use are key determinants of agricultural activity, incomes and personal security.'[18] It is therefore sobering to realise that neither the EC delegate in Kampala, nor senior officials in the East Africa Department of DGVIII, the EC's Directorate for Development Co-operation, expressed any concern that one indicator of the project's performance would be the number of people removed from forest areas. For the people removed from the Kibale Forest and Game Corridor, eviction meant the immediate loss of their homes, their livelihoods, their health, their personal belongings, their status, and their community. They were left traumatised and destitute.

Ugandan government inquiry into the evictions

Shortly after the event, the government set up a Cabinet Committee to conduct an inquiry into the Kibale evictions. In its final report[19] the Cabinet Committee identified four areas of concern:

- There had been a failure to give adequate, unambiguous notice of eviction.

- There was confusion over the territorial extent of the reserve; while the Cabinet Committee did not question the legality of the evictions, the extent of the applicability of the directive to expel those living 'in any part of a gazetted National Park, Forest and Game Reserve' left many unprepared for the subsequent expulsion.

- There was a lack of resettlement plans and compensation; although key personnel at District level felt that it was essential to identify alternative land before the evictions were carried out, their advice was not heeded.

- There were serious reports of the excessive use of force; the Committee accepted that some force was used during the evictions and called for further investigations to be carried out.

Many of those evicted had been encouraged and assisted by the colonial government officials to move to the Kibale Forest from Kigezi in the south-west of Uganda, one of the most densely populated and intensively cultivated areas in the country. Most settlers had lived in the Kibale Forest area for over 20 years. The government inquiry confirmed that some of those evicted were living inside the forest reserve, but the majority were living in the parish of Mpokya inside the Game Corridor (which was not part of the gazetted forest reserve).[20] The government set up a special inter-ministerial task force to examine the implications of the evictions, but, at the time of the operation in Kibale, it had not reported. The District Administrator of Kabarole apparently pressed ahead with the evictions without full cabinet approval.[21] The 30,000 people living inside the Game Corridor believed that they were safe from eviction, as the policy of the government of Uganda on environmental protection applied primarily to people living in gazetted forest reserves. However, on 31 March 1992, when the teams of Ugandan police and forest department officials began their operation, they evicted people from both the Game Corridor and the Forest Reserve.[22]

Alleged violations of human rights

The evictions were carried out by State agents and Kabarole District administration personnel. People were driven from their homesteads, their belongings were seized and driven away on lorries, then their homes and crops were burned or destroyed. The settlers' livestock and poultry were also seized. The Cabinet Committee Report concluded that 'the exercise was undertaken with inadequate and incomprehensive preparations under lack of proper guidance, political leadership and explicit instructions to follow'.[23] In fact, the only announcement of clear intent was a report broadcast on the radio a few days before the evictions began, which many of the settlers did not hear. The first notice most people had was when they saw the homes of their neighbours being set alight and armed police and civilians closing in on them, firing guns in the air.

We were chased out on the first day. I didn't know anything was happening until the police ran into my compound. They all had guns. They shouted at me, told me to run. I had no chance to say anything. They came at us and we ran, they came so violently. I was frightened for the children — I had eight children with me — but we just ran off in all directions. I took my way and the children took theirs. Other people were running, panicking, even picking up the wrong children in the confusion.[24]

While the government of Uganda should be congratulated for conducting a detailed inquiry into the Kibale episode, it is regrettable that, despite the recommendation of the Cabinet Committee's Report, these allegations were not subjected to a full investigation by the police. Most people evicted from the Forest and Game Reserve were left with nothing: their homes were burned, their livestock confiscated, their tools and utensils broken or looted, and their crops and food supplies destroyed.

The husband of one 22-year-old woman, Florence K., told Oxfam staff how she had been raped during the evictions, though she was pregnant. He had abandoned her because of the rape and because of his fear of AIDS. He later learned that she had miscarried and died alone in the bush. 'Of all the things that happened to me, that is what I most regret.' Settlers told Oxfam staff of other cases of rape, including that of young teenage girls. There were also a number of deaths attributed by the settlers to the evictions as a result of exhaustion, fear, malnutrition and exposure. No official estimate is available.

Responsibility for the violent and illegal manner in which the evictions were carried out clearly resides with Kabarole District Administration. But the EC cannot evade the charge that it agreed to finance this project, knowing that it would result in massive population displacement, and that it failed to make any provision either to compensate or resettle the affected communities, in contravention of the spirit and letter of the Lomé III Convention. It made no attempt to distinguish between short-term, opportunistic encroachers and those people whose only home and landholding was inside the forest reserves and game corridors. There is little doubt that the absence of any resettlement plan and the EC's refusal to provide prompt and adequate remedial assistance caused additional and unnecessary hardship.

Absence of resettlement plans

The scale of the displacement and the suffering it caused took many government departments by surprise. It was six months after the evictions occurred that resources were mobilised to help those who had been evicted. In August 1992, Oxfam was one of the first organisations to offer its assistance to the government of Uganda in the resettlement programme. The settlers were offered land in Bugangaizi County, Kibaale District, a remote and underdeveloped part of Uganda. The title to much of the land in Bugangaizi is in the hands of Buganda absentee landowners, but is leased or occupied by local Bunyoro people. Settlers have been given land in Nalweyo and Nkooko sub-counties; although they were promised title to this land, this is unlikely to happen. The District offered to resettle the people evicted from Kibale Forest Reserve and Game Corridor on the understanding that investment in infrastructure in Bugangaizi County would follow, to the benefit of both the settlers and the host community.[25] But neither infrastructure nor land-security has followed.

Kibaale District, formerly a part of Hoima, is situated in Western Uganda, with a population of more than 250,000 people. It was the sense of remoteness — it is as far from Hoima as it is from Kampala, the capital — and underdevelopment that led to its formation as a separate district in 1991. As a relatively new and isolated District, it suffers many disadvantages and it has a weak administration. Kibaale District is caught in a cycle of poverty. The District Administration has no funds to provide services for which it is responsible. Facilities such as feeder roads, primary health care, and primary education are not available or are of very poor quality. A baseline survey reports that 58.4 per cent of Kibaale's population has no formal education whatsoever. In terms of primary leaving examination results, Kibaale has the second-worst record of any District in Uganda.

Problems at the resettlement site

The first group of settlers arrived in Bugangaizi in September 1992. The 250-km journey from Kabarole District was then taking over three days by truck. No preparation had been made for the displaced people, and they spent over a month in the newly established camps. Disease was rife and the records provide evidence of a high incidence of anaemia, malnutrition, and kwashiorkor among settlers of all age groups.

Gradually families were allocated plots (but not titles), and the settlers moved out of the camps and began to build larger and more permanent shelters and to clear and develop the land. The emergency phase of resettling 15–20,000 people in Bugangaizi officially ended in May 1994.

The only contribution from the EC was 160 tonnes of rice to support a complementary food programme. For almost a year the Commission refused to contemplate any further assistance or to address the long-term needs of the settlers, arguing that the evictions were nothing to do with the project.

Despite the acknowledgement that in Kibale more people were truly landless and had nothing to fall back on after the eviction, the EC did not make any proposal to help the encroachers, because there was no resettlement component in the project, which was prepared before the OECD guidelines were issued. By 1992, however, the OECD guidelines were in force and new aid policies were in place, making poverty-alleviation and respect for human rights explicit aims of EC development co-operation. Prior to the eviction, the settlers had been able to feed themselves and produce a surplus for the market. The absence of a resettlement plan meant that they faced huge obstacles to regaining their former standard of living.

Long-term consequences

There is abundant empirical evidence to show that where displacement is poorly handled, severe impoverishment and social disintegration ensue, and heavy costs extend well beyond the immediately affected populations. The former Chief Sociologist of the World Bank, Michael Cernea, has identified eight characteristics of the process of impoverishment that occurs when people are forcibly displaced. They are *landlessness, joblessness, homelessness, marginalisation, increased morbidity, food insecurity, loss of access to common property resources,* and *social disarticulation.*[26] These are not the only impacts, only the most important ones. They are not mutually exclusive: different individuals experience them in differing ways, and they may occur with variable intensities in different locations. Delays in paying compensation reduce its value. Oxfam research has shown that it takes a number of years to restore incomes: where farm land and access to common property resources have been lost, resettlers may face increased costs. Merely restoring incomes does not compensate resettlers for the trauma and negative health impacts caused by involuntary displacement. All too often, people displaced by development projects are taken to be a homogeneous group. The basic differences in responses of particular groups of individuals to involuntary resettlement — that, for example, older people will find relocation more stressful than the young — are frequently overlooked. Gender-related aspects of resettlement are usually ignored.

Women displaced as a result of the Kibale evictions reported increased physical and social stress as a result of having to provide food for families while no longer having access to their own individual gardens. The vulnerability of children to disease and malnutrition in the aftermath of the evictions created additional stress for mothers. The workloads of female heads of households in resettlement areas increased, because they had to clear land and build their own houses. Because the evictions left women without a source of cash income, they were unable to pay male labourers to perform these tasks. Poorer settlers, widows, and female heads of households described their lives since the time of the evictions as years of 'begging, dependency and desperation'. Widows and single female heads of household constantly complain of being on their own and unable to cope with the demands of a settler's life. This isolation was felt particularly because of the amount of physical labour needed to clear virgin land, collect water from long distances, and construct their own homes.[27]

Several years after the evictions, the situation of the resettlers remains very difficult. The Uganda Rural Development and Training Programme — URDT, an Oxfam-supported NGO which has been providing support to the people evicted from Kibale — reports that the social infrastructure in Bugangaizi is very weak: schools are temporary buildings with grass-thatched roofs, and they suffer from a lack of teaching materials and suitably qualified staff. The host community and the settlers live in poor housing with poor and inadequate sources of water; they have limited access to markets, and to medical services and schools. They are caught in a vicious cycle of poverty: poor farming, lack of investment opportunities, and seasonal hunger.

Attempts by settlers in more remote areas to build their own schools have been thwarted by the difficulties of transporting cement, timber, and corrugated iron sheets, in the absence of feeder roads reaching deep into the villages. Many resettlement villages do not have access to safe drinking water. The resettlement areas have ill-equipped health posts, which often the villagers can reach only after a ten-mile journey on foot. These logistical problems ensure that infant mortality and maternal morbidity rates continue to be high. More than six resettlement villages along the Mpongo swamp are heavily infested with mosquitoes, and malarial deaths are on the increase.[28]

The Commission's response

Any project may have unforeseen consequences, despite best efforts at thorough preparation, consultation with local people, and careful monitoring during implementation. In the case of the EC's forest project in Uganda, both the preparation and the supervision were deeply flawed; and there was never any attempt to consult local people living in the forests and national parks.

When the financing agreement for the Natural Forest Management and Conservation Project was signed in 1988, the principles and objectives of the Community's aid programme were set out in the Lomé III Convention (General Provisions of ACP–EEC Co-operation). Lomé III legally required both the Commission and ACP governments to pay special attention to improving the living conditions of the poorest sections of the population. Article 4 states that the underlying principle for aid is to help 'promote the ACP States' social and economic progress and the well-being of their population through the satisfaction of their basic needs, the recognition of the role of women and the enhancement of people's capacities, with respect for their dignity'. A number of other important articles provide for local people's participation in project design and implementation (Article 116), for their basic cultural and physical needs to be met (Article 117), and for the cultural and social implications of aid to be taken into account at all the different stages of the operations (Articles 10 and 15). These provisions were disregarded by EC officials in the context of its forest project.

It was in October 1992 that Oxfam first raised with the Commission its concerns about the situation of the people evicted from the Kibale Forest. By the beginning of 1994, efforts by Oxfam and others over an 18-month period to obtain redress for the people evicted from Kibale were showing signs of success. In December 1993 pressure from Member States and Members of the European Parliament (MEPs) had led to the World Bank and EC sending a joint mission to investigate the situation in Bugangaizi. Senior officials in DGVIII had publicly promised that some remedial action would be taken to ameliorate the situation of the settlers.[29] The World Bank had also agreed in principle to make IDA funds available for key areas such as water supplies, roads, and health care, once the EC had identified the needs. In mid-1994 the EC commissioned a feasibility study to develop a development programme for Bugangaizi which was to benefit both the settlers and the impoverished host community. Taking these promises in good faith, Oxfam ceased its campaigning.

However, by the middle of 1995 Oxfam became concerned that the proposal had stalled. In fact, reports indicated that the Commission had shelved its plans to finance a remedial programme. These fears were confirmed in May 1996, when the Commission presented a Co-operation Strategy Paper to the EDF Committee, outlining its funding priorities for Uganda's next National Indicative Programme; it contained no reference to a rehabilitation programme for the Bungangaizi settlers. With no complaints mechanism available, Oxfam, URDT, and the Bugangaizi Settlers' Committee had little option but to take the matter to MEPs and enlist their support. Oxfam also took the unusual step of submitting a complaint to the UN Committee on Economic, Social and Cultural Rights, requesting it to decide on 'the advisability of international measures' taken by the World Bank and the EC in respect of the Kibale Forest evictions. Oxfam's case was that (given that Uganda had ratified the Covenant, and that many of the rights within the Covenant had been and continued to be violated, as a result of the failure of the donor agencies to prepare, implement, and supervise the project adequately or to take remedial measures to rehabilitate those people who were evicted) the role of the donor agencies fell within the scope of the Committee's powers 'to assist other UN organs in deciding on the advisability of international measures'.[30] Oxfam's version of events was largely substantiated by the officially commissioned Evaluation Report of the EC's Natural Forest Management and Conservation Report, which was published in July 1996. In October 1996, after leading MEPs had written to Commissioner Pinheiro and the Director General of DGVIII, Steffen Smidt, to express their concern about the situation in Bugangaizi, the deadlock was broken. A meeting was held between Mr Smidt, senior Commission officials, MEP Mrs Glenys Kinnock, and an Oxfam representative. The Director General gave his assurance that the Commission was prepared to consider funding, through its micro-credit programme, a community development project for the people evicted by the evictions from the Kibale forest.

Oxfam's Kampala office was subsequently invited by the EC Delegation to participate in an 'identification' mission to assess the needs of the settlers in Bugangaizi. In a welcome move, the EC made it clear that it would be willing to consider funding community development projects, but Oxfam was concerned that the ceiling of 300,000 Ecus would not be sufficient to restore the settlers to their former standard of living. The joint mission took place — at very short notice — in April 1997.[31] It could have achieved more, had the communities been given advance warning of the visit, so that discussions could have been held with them about their priorities. The joint mission spent one day driving through Bugangaizi to get a feel of the situation, when normally an identification mission would take several weeks. Surprisingly the joint mission did not use as a basis for the visit the results of the EC's 1993 Identification Study, which outlined priority areas for funding. Nor did the delegation refer to the 1994 consultants' report assessing the needs of the settlers, which had resulted in the Bugangaizi Community Development Project, envisaging EU support for the provision of education, health, roads, and water. The estimated cost of this project proposal was about $2 million. It is tempting to draw the conclusion that the earlier reports and recommendations were not used, not because the priorities had substantially changed, but because the EU might have been embarrassed by the contrast between the cost estimates and the level of support they were contemplating in 1994, when the Commission was under pressure from the European Parliament to undertake remedial action, and the limited amount it had decided to channel through Oxfam.

After the brief joint visit to Bugangaizi, the EU invited Oxfam to draw up a proposal for a small-scale community development programme worth not more than 300,000 ecus. The EU indicated that the approval process would be faster than normal (three-five months instead of more than one year). Oxfam Kampala agreed to work with the settlers and URDT to draw up a project proposal, which will focus largely on the settlers' need for safe water and education. Oxfam's Representative in Kampala expressed appreciation of the EU's willingness to support small-scale community projects, and he welcomed the improved working relationship which has developed between NGOs and the EC delegation staff. However, he pointed out that Oxfam had only limited funding available for this much-needed infrastructural work, which would greatly improve the quality of life not only of the settlers but also of the impoverished host community in Bugangaizi. Another impediment to more substantial development investments is seen to be the settlers' lack of secure tenure: titles to most of the land in the resettlement area are in the hands of absentee landlords. Despite the assurances given in 1992 by the government of Uganda that the settlers would be given title to land in Bugangaizi, this has not materialised. The EU Mission Report (25 April 1997) noted that 'a further problem lies in the attitude of the settlers in Bugangaizi County. It is a common view that the settlers have the right to be compensated by the government for losses of property incurred during the eviction from the Kibale Forest

Reserve and Game Corridor. Therefore, any development brought to the area from outside ... is considered part of the compensation expected and does not require any effort or contribution by the settlers.'

Underlying the Commission's response there seems to be a concern to dispel any notion that the EU itself shares some of the responsibility for the evictions from the Kibale Forest and Game Corridor — and, flowing from that, a duty to compensate the people for the losses they incurred and the hardships they have since had to endure. It is not possible to quantify most of the economic costs associated with the evictions which led to the loss of natural, human, social, and physical capital. The costs of resettling 15–20,000 people at Bugangaizi amounted to some $2 million. The Evaluation Report estimated that the value of the agricultural income lost in the first year after the evictions was about $2.04 million. Most of the people resettled in Bugangaizi lost at least one year's agricultural production. 'Even on the assumption that among the evicted households production levels after three years recovered to two-thirds of the pre-eviction levels, this implies a continuing annual loss of $0.68 million, which probably understates the losses.'[32] Furthermore these figures exclude the loss of personal property.[33]

Weaknesses in aid-management procedures were a contributory factor, as the evaluation report notes: 'The absence of a single complete project file in either DGVIII or the Delegation office in Kampala must have made it difficult for EC staff to comprehend the project and its activities.' Monitoring was minimal, and there appeared to be little pressure on the delegation to follow up on recommendations. For example, in May 1989 a prescient note to the Commission Delegate in Uganda from the Rural Development Technical Service in Brussels, raising concerns about the eviction of illegal squatters from forest reserves and wanting to know what arrangements had been made to assist them, was never acted upon: 'Although one can congratulate all those involved in the delicate operation of clearing the Forest Reserves from illegal squatters, I remain concerned about the approach which is one of law and order and perhaps one of force.'[34] One of the main conclusions of the Evaluation Report was that the social costs of the project could have been reduced, had parallel resettlement and development programmes been implemented.[35]

Conclusion

By the time the Natural Forest Management and Conservation Project came to an end in 1995, the 'exclusionist' approach to forest conservation which it had promoted was largely discredited. The subsequent evaluation criticised the project on a number of grounds. It noted the failure of the Commission to recognise the impossibility of maintaining forest control by a policy of excluding people. The costs of resettling encroachers evicted from the Forest Reserves should have been borne by the project. The project activities of boundary planting and the planting of previously encroached areas were neither cost-effective or financially sustainable. The long-term effectiveness of patrols in protecting the forest from non-agricultural uses is also in doubt. The report concluded that boundary demarcation and patrolling were not effective, because they simply do not address the underlying problems of poverty and the lack of alternative economic activities outside the forests. It was critical of the fact that the social costs of the project could have been reduced, if parallel resettlement and development programmes been implemented. It would have been possible to introduce a more participatory style of forest management and to adopt a more flexible 'process approach' to project management.

The practice of exclusion has alienated local communities surrounding Uganda's forest reserves. The social costs of eviction include increased vulnerability of some groups, inadequate resettlement provision, social insecurity incurred by displacement, and reduced access to health care and education services. Displacement without provision for resettlement has created new poverty and made many thousands homeless and landless. Whether or not one accepts the view that the Commission's whole approach to conservation was wrong, there can be little doubt that displacement without resettlement plans imposed huge and unnecessary costs on those least able to bear them. The lesson to be drawn is that no project or programme can ultimately succeed unless it reflects the perceptions and genuine needs and aspirations of local people.

This case leaves a lingering sense of injustice. It highlighted for Oxfam and others the need for Member States to set up an independent complaints panel to receive complaints from non-EU citizens. Such a body should have the power to recommend appropriate levels of remedial action for those who have incurred material harm as a result of failings in the management of the EU's development co-operation programme. The next chapter considers the effectiveness of existing accountability mechanisms.

DGVIII is taking steps to improve the quality of its aid programme by simplifying its procedures and introducing project-cycle management and the logical framework as management tools. But unless EU governments are willing to provide additional funds, there is little hope in the foreseeable future of reducing workloads at the Commission, or recruiting staff with appropriate skills to ensure that environmental, gender, and social issues are properly integrated into all its development-co-operation activities. Nevertheless, more can be done immediately to reinforce staff awareness and training in relation to basic principles of good aid practice and the safeguarding of fundamental human rights.

5   Accountability mechanisms

To be a good partner, we must be ready to listen to criticism and respond to constructive comment. There is no place for arrogance in the development business ... I want to have a Bank which is open and ready to learn from others — and which holds itself accountable. In that context, I regard our independent Inspection Panel as a valuable asset. (James Wolfensohn, World Bank President, address given to the Board of Governors at the 1995 Annual Meetings)

Introduction

One measure of a good aid programme is the ability of donors and the implementing agencies to recognise problems and take corrective action. Where actual material harm has occurred, as an unforeseen consequence of a development project or programme, remedial action should be taken to compensate those adversely affected. By this measure, most aid programmes would be regarded as deficient. Poor communities and individuals whose quality of life has suffered as a result of poorly conceived and executed projects are constrained by several factors in their attempts to claim effective redress; among these factors are top–down planning, inflexible project frameworks with rigid time limits, and a lack of clarity about the division of formal responsibilities between the donor, the borrower government, and implementing agencies or sub-contractors. While development may bring benefits at a national, regional, or — in the case of environmental projects — global level, the costs of such interventions all too often have been borne by local — generally poor — people. One practical step to ensure that projects or programmes are sensitive to local people's views and needs is to provide mechanisms for conflict-resolution, arbitration, and, where necessary, redress. Entitlement to a fair hearing and a just remedy is, after all, the necessary corollary to participation.

The World Bank's Inspection Panel

In September 1993, the World Bank made legal history by establishing an Inspection Panel to consider claims from those suffering 'a material adverse affect' as a result of Bank-funded projects, in the case of the Bank's own failures or omissions when applying its policies and procedures. The significance of the establishment of the Panel was far-reaching. Firstly, and for the first time, complaints from private actors against an international organisation could be heard before an investigatory body. Previously, international organisations were directly accountable only to their member States. The World Bank procedure established a direct relationship with affected parties that was distinct from the relationship between member State and the World Bank, or between State and citizen. Secondly, although the Panel is not a judicial body, its findings have the potential to influence the development of policy and practice.

Given that most financial assistance, even at the project level, can have such a profound and differential impact on the lives of poor people, the Panel procedure may be able to assist Bank management and borrower governments to determine their joint responsibilities for implementation.

The Bank's guiding rule has been to respect State sovereignty by making sure that it is the borrower who is legally responsible for implementation in all Bank loan agreements. However, the fact remains that how the Bank negotiates, structures, and administers loans has an impact upon the lives of millions. Hence its own operational directives and rules that govern how the process works are of vital importance, especially given the fact that the Bank staff, and in particular its Board of Executive Directors, are overwhelmed by the number of loans that must be approved and evaluated. In these circumstances, enormous power resides in the hands of the bank staff, who do all of the ground work on a loan proposal before it goes before the Board of Executive Directors, nominally the decision-making organ of the Bank. The latter, in the past, has been criticised for merely rubber-stamping staff decisions in most circumstances. The influence of the staff has been the more profound because no independent channel existed through which alternative opinions and information could reach the Directors. Once a loan was approved, its administration and disbursement was further controlled by unaccountable Bank staff.

Two imperatives arose against this background. The first concerned demands from non-government organisations, legislators, and member governments of the World Bank for increased public accountability. Many of these had been critics of the Bank's large-scale development projects such as POLONOROESTE and had been pressing the Bank to take more account of issues of social justice, environmental protection, and respect for human rights before agreeing to fund projects. The second related to the management of the Bank's portfolio and was driven by considerations within the Bank.

Critics in the first instance pointed to the distancing of the Bank from the concerns of those most directly and adversely affected by its funding decisions. The case of the Bank's approval of a loan of $450 million for the funding of the Sardar Sarovar Projects on the Narmada River in India illustrated the strength of this argument. There was widespread opposition to the construction of the associated dam and canal project, which was calculated to require the relocation of some 250,000 people and the expropriation of 117,000 hectares. International pressure on the Bank forced it to appoint an independent commission (the Morse Commission), which reported in 1992. It concluded that the Bank had violated its own rules and procedures in terms of the decision to lend and the disbursement of the loan. The Bank failed to ensure that the Environmental Impact Assessment was completed and did not enforce a loan provision requiring the Indian government to provide compensation payments before relocation. The Morse Commission Report prompted a Bank-wide review, which acknowledged the Commission's central criticisms.

The second key development was the 1992 Wapenhans Report, an internal review of the Bank's loan portfolio, which showed the proportion of problem projects or poor-performing projects to be significant and increasing. Overall, a preoccupation with promoting new loans of a less than consistent quality, rather than ensuring strict implementation and monitoring of existing loans, was to blame for the failures. In effect, loan agreements, as the most important public document, could not be relied upon to give an accurate reflection of the situation pertaining to a particular loan as it was actually administered. The implications of this for public accountability and impartial assessment were clear: it confirmed the suspicion that the Executive Directors were themselves often required to make decisions based upon inadequate information.

The Executive Directors, after a period in which alternatives were debated inside and outside the Bank, took three significant steps to improve accountability. Firstly, loan monitoring and evaluation procedures were tightened; secondly, they sought to make the work of the Bank more transparent, releasing more project information, including a 'Project Information Document'; and thirdly, as recommended in the action plan, a Resolution was adopted in September 1993, establishing an Inspection Panel.

The Panel's role, given the existence of already operational systems within the Bank for project monitoring, was to be limited to those exceptional cases where the Bank's own high standards were not met. It was therefore to act as a safety-net in the last resort and should be seen to complement rather than duplicate the function of the Bank's other supervisory procedures.

Comparable mechanisms were established in the regional development banks, such as the Inter-American Development Bank (IDB) and the Asian Development Bank (ADB). The World Bank Inspection Panel offered a number of clear advantages over the inspection mechanisms of the ADB and IDB, both of which opted for a roster of experts from which the Boards select a panel to investigate a particular complaint. Under the World Bank system, with a standing panel, the Board was able to reassure potential claimants that criteria and procedures adopted for investigation would be consistently applied. The World Bank Inspection Panel also had a greater degree of independence than the IDB procedure. Unlike the World Bank's Inspection Panel, which initially screens complaints, at the IDB it is the Board of Directors which first decides whether an investigation is warranted, based on a review of the complaint and management's written response.

Initial misgivings

Although strongly supporting the introduction of independent and effective scrutiny of Bank projects, when the Inspection Panel was first set up Oxfam feared that, as constituted, the Panel would be neither effective nor fully independent. From the outset, critics emphasised flaws in the general parameters within which the Panel operated. Oxfam was concerned about the fact that the approval of the Board was required before the Panel could undertake a full inspection. The Panel's remit was further circumscribed because it was able only to make recommendations and forward findings in relation to a claim. It was debarred by the terms of the Resolution from demanding compliance or redress. Such decisions were the sole prerogative of the Bank's Executive Board of Directors, who are ultimately responsible for the Bank's operations. The Panel was, paradoxically, both a creation of the Executive Board and, as recognised in the defining Resolution, an independent entity. The Panel has faced increasing difficulties in fulfilling its mandate. Institutional bias in the minutiae of procedure in favour of vindicating the Bank management often stemmed from these controlling parameters.

Within the Bank, there were are fears that the Panel would discourage a liberal interpretation of Bank procedures and a willingness to take risks; would interfere with the role of the Board or management; and might trigger a large volume of frivolous complaints at considerable cost. Rules to minimise such risks weakened the rights of complainants in the process, making it difficult for them to have their arguments heard. The Bank is open to the charge that, having invited people to air their grievances, it has since sought to exclude them from full participation in decisions that affect their lives.

Current practice

People who have been adversely affected by a Bank-funded project can request the Inspection Panel to investigate the matter. Provided that the alleged harm stems from the Bank's failure to adhere to its own operational policies or procedures, the Panel can recommend to the Board of Executive Directors that an investigation be launched into the Bank's management of a project. The Panel itself carries out any subsequent investigation and reports its findings to the Board of Executive Directors. The Board, after considering the response of the Bank management to the findings of the investigation, then makes a decision on what action, if any, is to be taken.

At face value, the establishment of the Panel offered many advantages over existing Bank monitoring methods. It promised the opening up of a dialogue between the Bank and those adversely affected by Bank projects — improving understanding on both sides — and an advance warning of problematic projects for the Board of Executive Directors at an early stage. It promised the involvement of ordinary people with a guaranteed channel of complaint when things went wrong; and it promised to make staff accountable for failures. Ultimately, by improving transparency and creating a public record, it opened up the possibility of influencing Bank procedure in the wider arena.

In practice the Panel has been hampered in its work by pressure from both Bank management and the Executive Directors. Despite this, it has sought to develop a manner of working which has attempted to balance the competing demands from all parties and has been seen to be even-handed in its approach. The first (and only) Panel investigation, into the Arun III Hydroelectric Project in Nepal in August 1995, contributed to the decision of the Bank to withdraw from a capital-intensive scheme to build a dam which threatened the livelihoods of people in the remote Arun Valley itself and which would have drained resources away from social spending at a national level. But since then Oxfam has been concerned that there has been a tendency to alter the parameters of the Resolution, to reduce the scope of the Panel's mandate, and to introduce procedural changes without prior notification to interested parties. In effect, the inspection mechanism has not been allowed to function in the way envisaged by the Resolution and approved by the Board. This has gradually eroded confidence in the independence of the Panel mechanism.

The Rondônia request for inspection

The first clear signs of the way in which the mandate of the Panel and its procedures could be altered unilaterally by the Bank management and the Board soon became apparent. The Rondônia request was filed by the NGO Forum in June 1995. The treatment of the Rondônia claim revealed a procedural bias towards institutional consultation and away from discussion with the complainant. The very terms of the Resolution establishing the Panel were modified by the Bank's Board when 'informal' changes were made, without consultation or prior public notification, to exclude the consideration of claims against the action of borrowers *and* Bank staff relating to procurement and the use of consultants.

After Bank staff, in their initial response, disputed the eligibility of the complainants, the Panel paid a preliminary review visit to the project area to substantiate the validity of claim. At this stage in the proceedings the Panel is not permitted to investigate management's actions in depth, but it is allowed to determine whether the failure to comply with the Bank's policies and procedures meets certain key conditions: that such failure has had or threatens to have a material adverse effect; that the alleged violations of the Bank's policies and procedures are serious; and that the remedial actions proposed are adequate to meet the concerns of the Requesters. In August 1995 the Panel submitted its report to the Board, recommending that it authorise an investigation. The Rondônia case illustrates the constraints on the Panel in its attempts to carry out an independent and thorough examination of complaints.

The Board postponed its decision on whether to authorise the Panel to conduct an investigation. Instead it diverged from the agreed procedures and requested the submission of additional material from the Panel 'to further substantiate the materiality of the damages and to establish whether such damages were caused by a deviation from Bank policies and procedures'. NGOs strongly suspected that the Board's indecision was a reflection of its willingness to sideline the Panel in order to protect Bank management from the embarrassment of an independent inspection. The delays gave the Bank's Brazil country team time to draw up their own remedial plan. The Executive Directors signalled their strong support for this approach by welcoming the Brazil Department's proposed supervision mission and the commitment to submit periodic progress reports on the project to the Board. In December 1995 the Panel submitted its 'Additional Review' to the Board, which maintained that a full investigation was still appropriate. But the Board had already weighted the scales against the Panel by restricting its additional review to the past (i.e. from the start of the project until the filing of the Request). Bank management, on the other hand, was able to submit its own up-to-date status report and a future plan of action which, it argued, made an investigation by the Panel unnecessary. No attempt was made to allow the Panel to assess the adequacy of the Bank team's assessment or plan. Nevertheless the Board ruled out a full investigation and accepted the Bank's proposal. The NGO Forum of Rondônia was highly critical of the Board's decision. The Board thanked the Panel for its 'invaluable insight and thorough assessment of the issues'.[1] As a concession to NGO concerns, the Panel was invited to review progress in implementation over the next six to nine months. Despite the fact that PLANAFLORO was supposed to be a participatory project, neither local NGOs nor the beneficiary groups had been consulted about the plan. They complained that there were no clear agreed benchmarks for monitoring implementation and that critical components of their claim were not even addressed.

The action plan

The action plan was mainly elaborated during the Bank's extensive emergency supervision mission between September and October 1995. At that time relations between the Bank and the NGO Forum were extremely tense, due in large part to the project team's resentment over the Inspection Panel claim. This only reinforced the Bank's existing tendency to negotiate primarily with government agencies during supervision missions, by-passing participatory institutions and keeping contacts with NGOs to a minimum. The quality of the action plan was further weakened by the fact that management took such a defensive position in reacting to the request for inspection, frequently denying the existence of problems altogether. This put Bank management in a rather difficult position: it found itself unable to include measures in the action plan to correct problems whose existence it had denied to the Board. In a letter to the President of the World Bank, soon after the Board's refusal to approve the Panel investigation on PLANAFLORO, the Rondônia NGO Forum requested a participatory revision of the action plan in order to take proper account of its concerns. The Forum also proposed a strategy for the independent monitoring of its implementation, but its proposal was never adopted.

After a few months the implementation of the action plan was thrown into complete disarray by a series of measures adopted by the government of Rondônia. The State Governor, bowing to pressure from the State logging industry, signed a decree which opened up commercial logging without any management plan within areas zoned for non-timber forest extraction (zone 4). As Oxfam had warned the Board, the State government, taking advantage of changes in procedures for demarcation procedures introduced by the Federal government, also attempted to reduce four indigenous reserves whose areas had been demarcated with funds from PLANAFLORO. There was further evidence of irregularities in the use of project funds, with excessive expenditure being recorded for road paving, to the detriment of environmental protection and community-development programmes. These violations of the loan agreement, in the immediate aftermath of the quashing of the Inspection Panel inquiry, created considerable disquiet among Bank staff. The Bank started to take a tougher line: for example, it immediately required the government to withdraw its appeals for the reduction of the Indian reserves. In April 1996, with the implementation crisis deepening and the threat of further damage to the Bank's reputation, management hastily hired a group of consultants to conduct the long-overdue mid-term review of PLANAFLORO.

Fears for the effectiveness and independence of the Panel, which became apparent during the discussions around the Rondônia claim, have subsequently been borne out. Extra-procedural practice has continued to impinge upon both the Panel's desired impartiality and the nature of its final recommendations. The Board has shown great reluctance to authorise investigations, almost invariably preferring to accept at face value the promise of 'in-house' action by Bank management. Confidence in the even-handedness of the procedures has been further undermined by the continuing prevalence of *ex parte* communications. *Ex parte* communications — one-sided communications from Bank management, which has privileged access to the Board — have had an undue influence on the final decisions.

In nearly all the subsequent cases in which the Panel, after the initial review stage, has made recommendations to the Board for an inspection, the Board has either postponed taking any decision (so as to avoid taking a vote) or vetoed an inspection altogether, irrespective of the merits of the case. This has fuelled suspicion that the Board is unwilling to follow the terms of its own procedures, as set down in the Resolution, and that its main aim is to protect the interests of the Bank at the expense of the rights of the complainants and integrity of the Inspection process.

The Board's decision on the PLANAFLORO project, which effectively usurped the Panel's role, was very controversial. After two years of poor implementation and two previous status reports, all faith in the Bank staff's ability to correct problems in Rondônia had evaporated. It was clear that the action plan had been prepared to stave off the pending investigation, yet it was not made public until after the Board meeting, giving the complainants no time to register their views as to its viability. There had not been adequate prior consultation on the plan with local NGOs and beneficiary groups. The Board, as a concession to the complainants, invited the Panel to participate in a review of progress within nine months. It soon transpired that the action plan was little more than a manoeuvre to allow the Bank more time to set in train corrective action and to avoid any potentially embarrassing independent oversight or findings. The Brazil staff resented the intrusion of the Panel. As a result of this failure to co-operate with the Inspection Process, the claimants had to wait another 12 months before PLANAFLORO — following a Mid-Term Review in June 1996 — underwent a major restructuring. (In March 1997, the Panel's report found mixed results: contrary to project objectives, deforestation during the period 1993–96 increased considerably; there were inherent difficulties in achieving most of the project's environmental goals; persistent invasions of indigenous and extractive areas had continued. However, the Panel acknowledged that Management supervision had improved. Despite the problems, the Panel noted that the locally affected people considered project continuation preferable to ending World Bank involvement.)

Obviously there would be no objection if an inspection was no longer necessary, because the Bank, after being informed by the Panel of a *bona fide* complaint, admitted the error and provided the complainant and the Panel with a remedial action plan to correct it. But NGOs and project-affected communities have become increasingly sceptical about the Board's uncritical acceptance of the adequacy of Bank management action plans, irrespective of whether or not they have met with the prior approval of the Panel and the complainants. While the complainants may, if they remain dissatisfied, pursue their complaint before the Panel, as in the Rondônia case, valuable time is lost and confidence in the integrity of the procedure is undermined. Richard Bissell, the former Chair of the Inspection Panel, expressed concern that 'Management is able to dominate the process through action plans, thereby diminishing the role of the Requesters'.[2]

Bank management has dismissed NGO criticism that the Panel is fundamentally flawed because it is unable to make its own decisions on whether investigations are warranted, and unable also to offer relief to complainants as a result of such investigations. It points out that the Bank's rules require that decisions be made by the decision-making organs of the Bank, which are defined in its Articles of Agreement. 'The Panel is not one such organ. Its intervention in operational matters by the issuance of binding decisions would conflict with the Bank's present governance structure and could cause serious problems to the management of its business.'[3] So, although the Panel is not an advisory body, it is an investigative body whose main function is to investigate complaints and come to a conclusion on whether the Bank has observed its policies and procedures. As the Bank's General Counsel goes on to explain: 'Such findings, while legally not binding on the Bank's decision-making organs, will undoubtedly have an overwhelming impact.' The Board, by routinely rejecting the Panel's recommendations for an inspection, is not only obstructing the Panel in its primary investigative role, but is employing administrative means to circumvent the exercise of the Panel's sole, formal prerogative, established in the Resolution, of coming to a finding. This has caused NGOs to question the value and relevance of the Panel procedure.

Review of the Panel

There was discernible unease among Southern Executive Directors, particularly as a result of the Rondônia claim, about the work of the

Panel, which some saw as a threat to national sovereignty. In fact the Resolution makes clear that the Panel has no authority to address the borrower or call on it to behave in any particular manner towards individuals or entities, and is exclusively charged with examining the Bank's actions and omissions. Nevertheless the Brazilian government complained that the procedure risked transforming a domestic dispute between the affected party and its government into an international dispute between the borrower government and the Bank. Nor did the Panel enjoy the wholehearted support of all the Northern Executive Directors. As a result, in September 1995, the Board decided to bring forward the planned review of the Panel's activities before the formal two-year deadline required by the Resolution. The review examined proposals to allow the Panel to conduct an assessment of material harm at the outset and if necessary extend the preliminary review time-frame. There was also concern to improve access to the mechanism by potentially affected people. The Board was also to examine whether and how other members of the World Bank group — the International Finance Corporation (IFC, the lending facility for the private sector) and the Multilateral Insurance Guarantee Agency (MIGA, which provides long-term non-commercial risk insurance to foreign investors) — could fall under the Panel's mandate. In October 1996, the Board completed the review and clarified aspects of the Resolution. A positive step was the decision to allow the Panel scope to undertake a 'preliminary assessment' of the damages alleged by the requester without having to seek full authorisation from the Board. But the Board rejected the notion that the Panel's mandate should be extended to include reviewing the consistency of the Bank's practice with any of its policies and procedures. The Board also continued to maintain sole authority for interpreting the Resolution and authorising inspections.

Since it was first set up, the Panel has received ten formal Requests for Inspection. Six of the claims related to failures to implement the Bank's policy on involuntary resettlement. Despite the specific reference in the Resolution and supporting documents to 'projects', the inspection procedure applies to other types of non-project loans, programme loans, and assistance. Only one such claim has been received. The other issues most frequently raised by Requesters concern environmental protection and the rights of indigenous peoples.

In November 1995, a Request concerning the Pangue/Ralco Complex of Hydroelectric Dams on the Bio Bio River in Chile was declared inadmissible. The people living in the project area, who included

Pehuenche Indians, complained that the IFC, which was part-financing the project, had violated a number of World Bank policies. The Panel argued that the Resolution establishing the Panel restricted its mandate to the review of alleged violations of operational policies and procedures related to the design, approval, or implementation of projects financed only by the IBRD or IDA. Although the Request was rejected by the Panel, Mr Wolfensohn in his capacity as the President of the International Finance Corporation instructed IFC management to conduct an impartial internal review of the project. In April 1997, a heavily edited version of this report (prepared by Jay D. Hair) was released; it criticised IFC for its failure to advocate 'the best and most advanced techniques for environmental management'. The Hair report commented that from 'an environmental and social perspective' IFC added 'little, if any value, to the Pangue Project'. The IFC's failure 'to supervise the project — from beginning to end — significantly increased the business risks and diminished the public credibility of the World Bank Group'. In particular the operations of the Pehuen Foundation — an innovative but experimental institutional arrangement established by the project to support programmes to benefit the Pehuenche people — was under-supervised by IFC. According to an Interim Evaluation of the Foundation, 'indigent beneficiaries' were 'systematically excluded from the Foundation programs'; and '20 per cent of the households received over half the Foundation's funds'. A work-voucher system 'excluded women-headed households, the disabled and the elderly and the most destitute'. Although some involuntary displacement of a small number of Pehuenche families was an inevitable consequence of the project, 'no resettlement plan had been prepared or contemplated'. The Hair report concluded that the Pehuenche participation was 'narrowly circumscribed'.   Given the rapid expansion of the World Bank Group's programme for private-sector lending and guarantees, Oxfam and other NGOs pointed out the desirability of the convergence of its supervisory procedures. Oxfam recommended that for the sake of consistency the Panel should be empowered to consider complaints relating to IFC and MIGA. A set of appropriate procedures could be developed to reflect private-sector concerns about competition and business confidentiality.

The Inspection Panel in crisis

The mounting hostility of borrower countries to the whole inspection process has come to the fore in recent months. In September 1997, opposition to the Panel's recommendation of an inspection of two projects, the Itaparica Resettlement Project in north-east Brazil and the Singrauli Power Generation Project in India, plunged the whole mechanism into crisis. The Brazilian government strongly objected to the Panel's recommendation of an inspection of the Itaparica project. Bank management denied that any policies had been violated, and the Board was split. In their desire to reach a solution, the Board accepted as satisfactory a last-minute assurance that the Brazilian government had drawn up its own Action Plan. The Itaparica project was the Bank's first free-standing resettlement loan. It was to have marked a sharp breakthrough in dealing with large-scale population displacement. Although the Bank had not completely financed construction of the Itaparica dam, in 1986 it had approved a substantial loan to the Brazilian energy sector. Completion of the Itaparica dam and the generating plant was one of the major on-going investments in the Brazilian power sector at the time. An explicit condition of the power-sector loan was that the Bank should ensure the resettlement and rehabilitation of 40,000 rural people forcibly displaced by the construction of the Itaparica dam in the lower Sao Francisco Valley. Members of the Inspection Panel conducted a preliminary assessment of the claim during a visit to the area in June 1997. They found that, ten years after the initial displacement and after 95 per cent of the loan had been disbursed, the situation for many remained desperate. Only 35 per cent of the irrigation projects had been installed; indigenous families were unable to grow crops, because the quality of their land was poor and the irrigation system was still in the design phase; many houses constructed in the resettlement sites were of poor quality; the delay in the installation and the commissioning of the irrigation projects — essential for the resumption of agricultural activities in the semi-arid zone of the north-east — had contributed to an increase in violence in the communities, to alcoholism and family breakdown. Despite calls from prominent members of the Brazilian Congress that the government should vote in favour of an inspection, the Requesters — the Polo Sindical, the rural trade union representing the resettled families — were told by the Brazilian Executive Director that matters concerning the Brazilian government should be discussed inside Brazil. But the Polo Sindical, supported by the Rede Brasil (a network of Brazilian NGOs which monitors the activities of multilateral develop-ment banks) insisted that the Request had nothing to do with an invest-igation into domestic affairs, but was rather an inquiry into actions or omissions by Bank staff. The whole purpose of the claim was to ensure a satisfactory outcome for the resettlement and rehabilitation project. The

Board rejected the Panel's recommendation for a full inspection after it had received reassurances from the Brazilian Executive Director that his government had prepared and was ready to implement its own Action Plan. This decision provoked a number of concerns: no one, neither the Board of Directors nor the Requesters, had prior sight of the government plan, which had been prepared behind closed doors; furthermore, although the Brazilian government promised to appropriate $290 million for completion of infrastructure and to provide technical assistance to local people, at a time of fiscal austerity it is by no means certain that the Brazilian Congress will approve this expenditure.

There is additional uncertainty. The Brazilian government, as part of its privatisation programme, is planning to sell off the regional power company which is responsible for the Itaparica project. The Polo Sindical and the complainants are uncertain whether a private investor could be required to carry out this remedial package. The Board, which has an important fiduciary role, was in the uncomfortable position of having vetoed an inspection when the feasibility of the Action Plan had not been independently assessed, and the finance had not been secured.

In the Singrauli case, the Board agreed to an inspection, but severely limited its scope. The Panel's role was reduced to carrying out a desk study. Once again the Board accepted another management action plan as a means of circumventing an effective independent investigation of the project by the Panel. But the repeated use of such discretionary options was never envisaged, either in the original Resolution or in the amended version. The Board of Directors, recognising that the whole process was in disarray, announced a further urgent review which should be completed in mid-1998. But, in the final analysis, once people adversely affected by Bank projects and programmes lose confidence that their claims will be given a fair hearing according to stable predictable rules, and that the Board is willing to accept the Panel's recommendations, then the whole Inspection process becomes tainted.

Whatever the limitations of the Inspection Panel, there is little doubt that, by making the operations of the World Bank more accountable and transparent to its grassroots constituents, it has 'altered the paradigm for governance of all international financial institutions'.[4] The Board has become less interested in examining the application of Bank policies and more interested in identifying and correcting damage to project-affected people. Although the Board has routinely rejected Panel requests for investigations, the Panel's intervention has helped to bring the Bank's work on the ground into line with its policy standards. The most noticeable impact of filing a claim is the extraordinary and immediate increase in project supervision. As the situation of the families evicted from the Kibale Forest in Uganda demonstrates, no similar mechanism of last resort exists for an independent assessment of alleged harm arising in the context of the EU's development co-operation projects and programmes.

Protection offered under the Lomé Convention

Negotiations are under way concerning the future of the EU's aid and trade agreements with developing countries. Oxfam believes that member states and the Commission should urgently address the weaknesses in the protection currently offered under the Lomé Convention. The failure to formulate and appraise a project adequately is at the heart of the question of redress. Since 1980 successive Lomé Conventions have incorporated principles committing the EU to upholding the basic rights of individuals and to protecting the environment.[5] Lomé III stipulated that development co-operation in African, Caribbean, and Pacific (ACP) States should promote the social and economic 'well-being of their population'; 'the satisfaction of their basic needs'; 'the enhancement of people's capacities'; and 'respect for their dignity'. Provision should be made for the cultural and social implications of aid to be taken into account at all stages of the operations and for local people's participation in project design and implementation so that their basic needs are met. It is further stipulated that project appraisal must consider 'the effects expected from the ... social ... and environmental viewpoints'. Lomé IV, covering the period 1990–2000, reinforces the message: co-operation through development 'shall help abolish the obstacles preventing individuals and peoples from actually enjoying to the full their economic, social and cultural rights'; and 'priority must be given to environmental protection'.

However, there is no clear indication about what should happen when these principles are not upheld. Firstly, under Lomé III, disputes between an ACP State on the one hand and Member States or the Community on the other over both the application or interpretation of the Convention are resolved by referral to the Council of Ministers or, if necessary, through arbitration. Should a party then fail to take the measures required for the implementation of the arbitrator's decision, no explicit sanctions are detailed under Lomé III; however, and in extreme circumstances, either the Community or the ACP State may denounce the Convention. Secondly, the Convention specifies how disputes between an ACP State and contractor should be resolved. Similar provisions exist under Lomé IV, and indeed were extended after a mid-term review.[6]

Two points need to be made about these provisions in respect of remedial action. Firstly, there is an implicit assumption — despite the formal power of both the Community or an ACP State to invoke remedial measures — that any failure to meet the principles in the Convention will be on the part of the ACP State and not on the part of the Community. After all, 'denouncement' of the Convention makes sense as a sanction only when it is applied against an ACP State. Such dual standards further the cause of those who argue that conditionality is incompatible with the desire for greater ownership of the development process. Oxfam believes that the EC must also look to itself and its own obligations in upholding the principles of the Convention. Secondly, because channels of remedial action are limited to redressing disputes and failures of obligation between the Community and an ACP State, people adversely affected by projects and programmes have no direct means of redress or compensation under the Convention. In short, if the EC fails to fulfil its own obligations under the Convention, and as a consequence the basic rights of local residents are undermined in the implementation of a project, then there is currently no clear-cut provision for them to raise the matter directly with the Community. At this point the Community's ostensible support for basic rights and poverty alleviation, declared in the Convention, is in danger of appearing merely rhetorical.

There is, however, a provision in the latest Lomé IV Convention that builds on a previous article in Lomé III and can reasonably be interpreted as applicable to both the Community and ACP States in the redress they offer to people adversely affected by a project. Article 10 is unequivocal in determining that action should be taken:

'The Contracting Parties shall, each as far as it is concerned in the framework of this Convention, *take all appropriate measures, whether general or particular, to ensure the fulfilment of the obligations arising from this Convention* and to facilitate the pursuit of its objectives. *They shall refrain from any measures liable to jeopardise the attainment of the objectives of this Convention.'* [Emphasis added]

Yet, despite this obligation, no specific measures of redress for third parties have been codified in any detail under the Lomé Convention. Unless Member States rectify this situation and set up an accountable chain of responsibility, the principles espousing human rights and poverty alleviation at the level of the individual and the local community in the Convention amount to little more than empty rhetoric. The EU has acknowledged that shared responsibility in managing aid between the Commission and the beneficiary countries has been a source of confusion and delay. 'Despite improvements made in successive conventions, all evaluation studies show the cumbersome joint management system has hampered the effectiveness of aid'.[7] Oxfam has suggested that one way of translating the principles of transparency, accountability, and participatory development into specific action would be to set up an effective complaints mechanism. The current situation imposes an inordinate burden on project-affected people.

The Development Finance Co-operation Committee, which is a subsidiary body of the Council of Ministers, already has powers to examine specific problems at the request of the Community or the ACP States. While the Community can study problems of implementation 'with a view to facilitating the removal of any difficulties', Oxfam is unaware of any situation in which those adversely affected by a project have succeeded in having their complaint heard, let alone that they have obtained effective redress, at this level.[8] Given the relative weakness of the European Parliament (which, for example, in the case of the non-budgetised aid has no formal control over the European Development Fund), there is no means of ensuring that the political institutions heed the exhortations in the Maastricht Treaty to respect human rights.[9] Decisions on whether to finance specific projects are taken by another subsidiary body of the Council of Ministers, the EDF Committee, which is composed of senior civil servants from Member States. Control of the Community's finances is the responsibility of the Court of Auditors, which reviews all EU expenditure, including the cost-effectiveness of the Commission's development and humanitarian work. The Court of Auditors' reports, which have been critical of the aid programme, have been influential in changing spending priorities and improving accounting procedures. As an institution, however, the Court is less successful in following up on problems posed by specific projects. While the Parliament's Development and Co-operation Committee has the power to raise concerns about implementation of the EDF programme and to question Commission officials, the level of detailed knowledge about specific projects and programmes that is required inevitably puts even the most conscientious MEPs at a disadvantage. Since 1981 the European Parliament's rules of procedure have allowed for the setting up of *ad hoc* committees of inquiry. Article 138c of the Maastricht Treaty strengthened this provision, allowing the Parliament to establish a temporary inquiry committee 'to investigate alleged contraventions or maladministration in the implementation of Community law'. There is also an entitlement for both citizens and any person resident in or having their office in a Member State to petition the European Parliament (Article 138d, Treaty of Union). Community Institutions are also subject to the jurisdiction of the newly created Ombudsman (Article 138e, Treaty of Union), who is appointed by the European Parliament. The Ombudsman may examine cases of maladministration on the part of Community institutions — by which is meant administrative irregularities or omissions, abuse of power, and negligence. The institutions must supply information on request and give access to files, except where exemption on grounds of security is claimed. At the conclusion of the investigation, the Ombudsman is to send a report to the European Parliament and to the institutions under investigation, and the complainant is to be informed of the outcome. The Ombudsman also presents an annual report to the European Parliament. But once again the Ombudsman may receive complaints of maladministration by Community Institutions only from the same category of persons who may submit petitions. In January 1997 a complaint filed by a Kenyan MP, Mr Paul Muite, was rejected by the Ombudsman. He had written to the Ombudsman on behalf of several thousand poor people living on the outskirts of Nairobi who had been struggling for over six years to obtain compensation for damages incurred during an EDF-financed road-rehabilitation project for the Westlands–St Austin and Kabete–Limuru roads. A parallel complaint concerning the same project, the Great Northern Corridor Road Project in Kenya, filed by an individual EU citizen was, however, considered admissible and is still under consideration by the Ombudsman.[10] But at the end of this protracted process, even if the Ombudsman finds that the Commission had been negligent, it is Oxfam's understanding that, while he is entitled to make recommendations to institutions of the European Community, he has no formal powers to ensure that remedial action is carried out.

The problems which residents of Gitaru and Rungiri have experienced and continue to face resulted from the design of the highway and the manner in which the construction work was carried out. A quarry and stone-crushing plant was located in the vicinity of their homes and farmland. Residents suffered a decline in their living standards; their basic right to physical and mental health was violated, and many now suffer permanent damage to their lungs as the direct result of dust-inhalation. In short, people in both communities have been impoverished as a result of the road construction. Under Lomé III the Commission had joint responsibility to appraise the project and final responsibility for approving the Financial Proposal, which formed the basis of the Financing Agreement. A social and environmental assessment should have been carried out, and alternative solutions should have been examined. Despite repeated complaints from the residents about the impact of the project during implementation, the EC took no action to remedy the situation.[11] Some of the residents attempted to file claims in the Kenyan Courts against the contractors, FEDIMP (a Nairobi-based company in which the Italian holding now known as IMPREGILO was a prominent stakeholder at the time). But very few of the claims have been settled, and their cases will soon by time-barred. The poverty of the residents means that, even when legal representation is given *pro bono* and when lawyers agree to defer fees in exchange for a share of any settlement, filing fees are prohibitive and calculated as a percentage of the compensation, so the more that is claimed in damages, the higher the fee. Attempts to reach an out-of-court settlement have also stalled.

In October 1996, after pressure from a number of MEPs and the intervention of Mrs Glenys Kinnock, the Commission offered to finance a cluster of micro projects for the affected communities, once again setting a ceiling of 300,000 ecus. However, more than 18 months later, little progress has been made in drawing up project proposals.

Unlike the World Bank, which enjoys immunity from legal action before national courts (except where this is explicitly waived), the EU does offer one other potential avenue for project-affected people to seek redress. Article 215 of the Maastricht Treaty entitles even non-EU citizens to file complaints before the European Court of Justice (which oversees the proper application and interpretation of Community law) and to seek to recover damages caused by Community institutions or 'by its servants in the performance of their duties'. But all litigation is a lengthy, costly, and complicated, which explains why no cases concerning the Commission's development co-operation programme have been filed.

Oxfam believes that both the Ugandan and Kenyan cases have highlighted the need for the EU to have an independent complaints mechanism — similar to the World Bank's Inspection Panel — so that those people who have a *bona fide* complaint about inadequate preparation, appraisal, and supervision of an EU-financed project or programme, or alleged violations of the principles of the Maastricht Treaty and revised Lomé Convention, could be assured of a fair and prompt hearing. Contingency funds should be available to compensate those people adversely affected — without having to resort to complex government negotiations or waiting, sometimes years, for the next round of aid programming. In the public debate launched in 1997 by the Commission around its Green Paper on the future of its co-operation agreements with African, Caribbean, and Pacific countries, a growing number of European development and environmental NGOs, represented by the NGO Liaison Committee, have urged EU governments to give priority consideration to the establishment of a complaints procedure. As Mrs Kinnock, writing about the Kenyan and Ugandan cases, has pointed out: 'many of the problems we are now dealing with could have been minimised if complaints had been thoroughly examined and acted upon sooner'. In her view, a complaints mechanism could help the Commission and MEPs to assess grievances at a much earlier stage. 'If after an inquiry complaints were considered to be well founded, the complaints committee could make recommendations to correct damage to the local community. This procedure would obviously only be used in cases where problems have arisen and the EC Delegation and the alleged affected parties have been unable to resolve the matter through the normal channels.'[12]

One of the inherent weakness of existing grievance procedures is the fact that donor institutions, in their anxiety to avoid any suggestion of formal liability, usually restrict remedial action to community-wide small-scale development projects. Individual or household compensation is almost never an option. Of course, development literature is replete with examples to show that cash payments are an inappropriate method of compensation; however, there are obvious problems with the current community-level solutions. First of all, there are huge opportunity costs for a community in drawing up project proposals which meet the donors' requirements. Doing so almost inevitably requires support from an established intermediary, which has the effect of transferring responsibility for solving the problem from the Commission to an NGO. These remedial actions tend to become trammelled in wider government–EU aid negotiations and project cycles. In the Ugandan case cited in this book, for example, the Commission insisted that, since it had no contingency funds to draw on, remedial action would have to wait for the next round of the (five-yearly) national indicative programming. In the Kenyan case, those affected by the road construction were not a homogeneous or readily identifiable group. In these circumstances, it was unrealistic of the Commission to insist that remedial assistance could not be provided until the diverse and fragmented population living in the Nairobi suburbs had produced a cluster of interlocking micro projects. Secondly, community-level solutions are by their nature non-specific, which leaves open the possibility that the proposed remedies may not address or correct the residual harm suffered by particular, vulnerable individuals or households. The building of a school, for example, though desirable to the majority of people in a community, may not be of any direct benefit to an elderly widow bereft of adequate shelter or means of support. Thirdly, in the absence of baseline data, the lengthy delays that almost invariably occur between the infliction of the damage and agreement being obtained from the donor institution to finance mitigating measures mean that the task of identifying those who have suffered the greatest physical or economic losses becomes difficult and contentious. Finally, neither the World Bank's Inspection Panel nor the European Ombudsman is empowered to make recommendations; discretion thus rests in the hands of the project or programme managers, who may have been responsible for the damage in the first place, to determine the level and nature of the remedial action. In such a process, the needs and views of the injured parties are easily ignored.

In Oxfam's view, one of the most tangible indications of the EU's determination to overcome past difficulties in the effectiveness of its aid and its willingness to incorporate principles of transparency and accountability in its own operations would be the establishment of a complaints mechanism which recognised the rights of non-EU citizens. If the EU is genuinely interested in fostering participative approaches, it should recognise that the traditional closed governmental circuits that have typified its deliberations and decision-making processes will have to be opened up not only to EU citizens but to a wider public, including the intended beneficiaries of its development co-operation.

6 Extending participation and ensuring equity

Extending participation

The challenge confronting all those involved in development is to learn from the early experiences of participation at a project level and then to ensure fairness and equality across the whole range of government policies and programmes. As the case studies in this book have shown, participation is understood in different ways by different agents. In the early stages, participation — as in the PLANAFLORO project in Rondônia — was often cosmetic or manipulative: local NGOs or community representatives were given a formal role on steering committees, but had no real power to affect decisions. Or it was passive — as in the Forest Department's implementation of the Western Ghats Project in Karnataka, where key decisions about forming village forest committees and planting targets were taken in advance of any consultation. Participation in such cases plays a merely functional role: involving people only as a means of achieving pre-determined objectives at reduced costs.

Efforts to bring participation into the heart of economic and social planning have gathered momentum over the past five years. It is in this area that participation has been most often misconceived as a one-off consultation, where information is not provided in an adequate or timely manner and where proposals and reactions from civil-society organisations are not seriously considered. This is most apparent in the first consultations organised by the World Bank on specific Country Assistance Strategies (CASs). They arose as part of an effort by the Bank to make CASs more socially focused and poverty-oriented.[1] These experimental consultations on Country Assistance Strategies were initially limited to about six countries, whose governments had agreed to their taking place. But there has been some reluctance to extend CASs to include civil-society organisations, despite growing pressure on the World Bank and governments to open up the Country Assistance Strategies not only to the scrutiny of NGOs but to the active participation of civil society, in order to ensure that the Bank's priorities more closely reflect the priorities of the government and society as a whole.

The CAS is a fairly recent innovation: before 1995, planning documents for a whole country programme did not exist, and the focus tended to concentrate on individual loans.[2] (The CAS is the immediate descendant of the Country Strategy Paper, which in turn replaced the Country Program Paper.) The CAS often lays out ambitious reform objectives, and assesses macro-economic conditions, but tends to exclude analysis of underlying social and political forces that inevitably condition the feasibility, effectiveness, and sustainability of the programmes and projects that are being proposed. CASs have generally not incorporated participatory processes in their preparation. Consultations have tended to take place mainly between the Bank and the governments, with little or no attention given to the views of other interested and affected stakeholders, although the World Bank has begun to recognise that, if it wishes to ensure the sustainability of development programmes, the CAS will have to encourage the adoption of policies that promote equity in distribution of welfare and transparent, open political processes. Some World Bank staff acknowledge that insufficient account has been taken of the risk of social dislocation resulting from rapid economic policy change.

Predictably the introduction of participation has not been problem-free. In September 1996, for example, the World Bank held a meeting for NGOs in Maputo to discuss the CAS for Mozambique. The NGOs were then invited to submit written comments to the Bank about the document. The NGOs objected to the fact that they had not been consulted during the preparation of the CAS itself, but were presented with the document in its finished form in February 1996, only days before it was due to be presented to the Board in Washington. Oxfam recognises that, although the process was flawed, 'it represented a move on the part of the Bank in the direction of greater World Bank–NGO interaction'.[3] Oxfam questioned whether the CAS, which pointed to the potential for 'civil strife', had ensured that sufficient measures were in place to cushion vulnerable groups from 'the impact of the rising cost of living and steadily deteriorating purchasing power'. In El Salvador the process was similarly disappointing, with NGOs unsure even what the purpose of the consultation was.

Assessing impacts

NGO campaigns to broaden the concept of participation are informed by a number of different standards and experiences. In many industrialised countries, there have been serious attempts to conduct impact-assessments as part of the process of considering proposals for legislation or major policy initiatives. These go beyond environmental concerns and the limited approach of traditional anti-discrimination law, which applies generally to specific types of employment or service-provider. In Britain, guidelines exist which seek to integrate people affected by planning proposals into the policy-making process; but the potential of these guidelines (the Policy Appraisal and Fair Treatment guidelines) has not been explored by the voluntary sector. The PAFT guidelines, which are relatively little known outside government departments, place emphasis on the need 'to avoid unlawful discrimination (both direct and indirect) to ensure that there is no unjustifiable inequality or inequity and to incorporate a fair treatment dimension into public administration'.[4] The Commission for the Administration of Justice, an NGO working in Northern Ireland, believes that the PAFT guidelines, even if they were properly implemented, might not be able to prevent actions which increase material inequality, but would at least ensure that planning decisions were taken in the full knowledge of their consequences, and with public participation and accountability.

Informal guidelines on social assessments were belatedly introduced by the World Bank in May 1994. Many practitioners see social assessments as a means of providing a framework for incorporating participation and social analysis into the design and delivery of the Bank's operations. It is acknowledged that social assessments permit better orientation of projects towards the poor, and, when carried out early enough, they influence or change project design. Social assessments identify stakeholders, ensure that project objectives and incentives for change are acceptable, quantify social impacts and risks, and help to develop capacity at appropriate levels. A related approach, beneficiary assessments, involves consulting beneficiaries in order to identify and design development activities. Beneficiary assessments help to identify potential constraints on local people's participation in projects. Unfortunately a study of social and beneficiary assessments conducted by the World Bank since 1994 showed that the majority were not being done early enough to influence project design.[5] Of course, as earlier chapters have shown, NGOs have been conducting beneficiary assessments for years in their campaigns to obtain redress for the victims of bad development projects. Pioneering techniques like participatory poverty assessments, which include beneficiary assessments, have started to provide useful qualitative information, but according to the Bank the information could not always be used, because it 'lacked operational focus'. Participatory poverty assessments — the purpose of which is to draw up 'poverty profiles' of developing countries and identify appropriate actions for poverty alleviation — may not yet have had the impact on the World Bank's policy formulation that Oxfam would like, but they point the way to the future. In Zambia, the participatory poverty assessment carried out in late 1993 is credited with prompting the World Bank to change the priorities of its lending programme to take into account the importance to the poor of rural infrastructure and the continuing problems with the delivery of education services.[6]

Decentralisation and civil society

While the early experiences of participatory development have had mixed results, the approach continues to be officially endorsed and promoted by the World Bank and most official donors. Just as no project or programme exists in isolation, but is shaped by wider political, social and economic forces, so too participation is conditioned by the prevailing context. Where there has been a tradition of democratic government, or there is a commitment to reform, participation can have a dramatic impact. Where favourable social and political conditions do not obtain, it is idle to expect participation to work miracles. According to the Inter American Development Bank, 'participation in development is gaining strength because the environment for it has never been more fertile'.[7] This is true particularly in Latin America, where there has been a definite shift to democratisation and the decentralisation of power from central to local governments.

Measures like the Popular Participation Law in Bolivia, which was introduced in 1994, are helping to address problems of exclusion from public discussion and the government's lack of administrative capacity. Some 42 per cent of the Bolivian population, Indians and peasants, lived in remote rural communities where there was no official government structure or presence. They lacked the resources necessary to meet their basic human needs. State resources were concentrated in Bolivia's economic centres, La Paz, Cochabamba, and Santa Cruz, which received 90 per cent of municipal tax revenue. The Popular Participation Law promoted a programme of decentralisation by creating new municipalities which have control of and responsibility for health, education, and local infrastructure. The Law cannot immediately correct the imbalance and inequities entrenched by centuries of oppression ar d neglect, but it offers the possibility of increased participation by all o Bolivia's citizens in decisions and activities that affect their daily lives.

Too often, however, decentralisation has meant handing over the burden of social provision to local authorities without simultaneously allowing them full decision-making power or providing sufficient transfer of resources. 'The state is handed an excuse to relinquish its basic responsibilities onto the laps of cash-starved, overextended local governments and grass roots organisations.'[8] The Food and Agriculture Organisation warns that this may be happening with the rushed process of decentralisation in sub-Saharan Africa, where the factors affecting the process are 'often not rational, predictable or logical'.[9] In sub-Saharan Africa, FAO sees a limited form of decentralisation emerging, in which command is retained by the central authority by means of political appointees who head local administrative units. In Zambia, decentralisation has been introduced 'in a blanket fashion without giving time for assimilation and adaptation'.[10] In some sub-Saharan countries, planning activities have been marginalised to a ritual; policy making is confined to a narrow elite circle; plans often constitute a catalogue of *ad hoc* projects. In others, planning is simply being done abroad. The FAO study recommends, in view of the improbability of a quick realignment of the planning and decision-making processes, an incremental, selective, and sequential approach which aims to enhance local administrative capacities and resources.

At its best, decentralisation can give people a sense of the importance of working together to confront their problems directly. It can encourage the development of local leadership and give poor people training in management practices. In 1989, the city of Porto Alegre in Brazil adopted a radical approach to addressing the problems of severe budget shortfalls and limited access to resources, by designing a mechanism to broaden participation in the budget process. The *Orcamento participativo* — the participatory budget — developed under the municipal administrations controlled by the Workers' Party in Brazil — is seen by many as an example of a genuine decentralisation of social policy. The citizens of Porto Alegre participated directly in the decision-making process, in terms of both defining government policies and determining how money was to be spent. It is estimated that over 100,000 people were linked to the creation of the city budget. Between 1989 and 1995, about $700 million were disbursed for local priorities, following the participatory budget process. Over this period, the provision of water and sanitation services increased significantly, and during the first five years of the participatory process the number of children enrolled in public schools doubled.[11]

Promoting equity in policy-making depends on the ability of all parties to participate. It requires a degree of confidence and trust among the participants: NGOs should not simply treat it as a way of obstructing change; nor should those in power regard it as a mechanical exercise with no real attempt to accommodate the priorities of the least advantaged. Brazil's 1988 Constitution paved the way for decentralisation and participation, but UNICEF quickly recognised that the general public finds the public budget difficult to understand because of its technical nature. If people's participation was going to work, the process had to be demystified. UNICEF has supported work to improve the capacity of NGOs, State officials, local councillors, and others in order to equip them to understand and participate in the budgetary process.

In north-east Brazil, the municipalities have had a very limited scope for action. In the majority of rural municipalities the local administration has not had the capacity to tackle the challenge of its development effectively. Traditionally the municipalities have been regarded as passive institutions, almost always without financial resources or an adequate tax base. For this reason, perhaps, many still act as bodies dependent on central authorities. But this is not always the case. The north-eastern State of Ceará, with 6,700,000 inhabitants, is in one of the poorest and most arid regions of Brazil, but encouraging changes have started to occur, particularly in response to a campaign supported by UNICEF on the rights of the child.[12] In the space of just three years (1987–90), infant mortality rates were reduced from 95 to 65 per thousand live births. Similar improvements were noted in levels of mal-nutrition among children under the age of three years (12.8 per cent to 9.6 per cent). There was a significant improvement in vaccination coverage and the use of oral rehydration techniques.[13] The situation has continued to improve, thanks to collaboration between governmental agencies, NGOs, and the private sector. The new positive climate in the relations between State and municipalities and the process of decentralisation were determining factors, as well as the growing transparency in the way in which public authorities took decisions. The functioning of State and municipal councils on issues related to health and to children played a crucial role. Representatives of service-providers and State officials, as well as users of the services and NGOs, all participated in the councils. Community-level action also played an important part: in particular two large-scale programmes on community health agents and community crèches helped to spread and improve demands for services from the population, as well as making families more capable of protecting their children's health and development. A communications campaign using local radio stations has been crucial to the positive results of the programmes. UNICEF also helped to set up monitoring systems which have become efficient tools for mobilising action.

However, without the presence of a central State with the political will to correct inequalities, decentralisation ends up excluding the weakest social groups. Research generally supports the view that the success of decentralisation depends on the context, especially with respect to socio-economic conditions and the strength of civil society. In less enlightened parts of Brazil, devolving power to local municipalities has simply ended up as *prefeiturisação* — a situation in which the local mayor and a circle of advisers dominate decisions about resource allocation. So, although decentralisation may bring power closer to people, it does not necessarily make it more accessible to them. Local participation always requires some form of decentralisation, but the reverse is not true. In a study of Oaxaca's Municipal Funds Programme, researchers found that State officials significantly influenced project choices in 38 per cent of municipalities. There was also a tendency for officials to encourage communities to choose projects for which they had a standardised formula. Active community participation in project selection and implementation is a necessary but far from sufficient condition to produce a positive impact on poverty. Research has also shown that it is wrong to assume that decentralisation alone will encourage greater accountability. The impact of decentralisation on accountability depends on the degree to which local government was representative before it received additional external resources.[14]

Signs of progress

What were the factors that made Porto Alegre's participatory budget and Ceara's campaign to improve the health of young children so successful?

They include the following:

- a shared common purpose among the different institutions and stakeholders;
- a genuine enthusiasm for the objectives of the project;
- the delivery of tangible benefits within a reasonably short time - frame;
- the use of a media strategy to disseminate relevant data on progress and to maintain momentum;
- and, finally, the wholehearted support of the State governments, which created an enabling context in which participation and decentralisation could flourish.

Clearly not all of these factors are present in the complex situations in Karnataka and Rondônia, and so, despite the best efforts of DFID and the World Bank, who are working hard to improve the quality of local participation, there are ominous signs that centrally determined large-scale developments may undermine the aims of the participatory approach to natural-resource management which their projects are trying to foster.

Karnataka

The State government of Karnataka is heavily promoting tourism, and several large hotels are being planned in Uttara Kannada, the most ecologically important area of the Western Ghats. Industrial developments are also on the Government's agenda: a number of energy and transport projects are under way which will inevitably increase pressure on the forests and on the livelihoods of local people. These investments are likely to have a detrimental effect on the possibility of sustainable forest management. In October 1997 over 3,000 environmental activists, including tribals from all districts of Uttara Kannada, attended a rally to protest against the large-scale development projects planned for the district. They submitted a memorandum to the Deputy Commissioner, expressing concern that these projects would largely benefit 'elite outsiders' and would deprive local poor people of their access to the District's abundant natural resources. The memorandum called upon the State government to stop 'mega development projects' which were leading to deforestation, and it called for a greater role in decision making about the use of these resources through the Joint Forest Planning and Management Process. While the arguments about growth versus conservation and equity will continue, potentially the emphasis on participation that DFID has tried to promote in the Western Ghats Forest Project will be seen to have strengthened the negotiating skills of local people and may lead to their exercising greater influence over development priorities. But DFID has been markedly less successful in encouraging the government of Karnataka to adopt a sustainable approach to the management of forest resources which could maximise the benefit to the livelihood needs of local communities. Nor has it really been able to secure the change of institutional culture inside the Forest Department, which still clings to its 150-year-old policing traditions.[15]

Rondônia

In Rondônia, the World Bank faces an even greater challenge. It is making efforts not only to help to alter the focus of PLANAFLORO but also to promote participatory planning throughout the State.[16] The aim is to help to build a consensus with all relevant stakeholders on developing a strategic plan for the State. If successful, it will provide a blueprint for more sustainable approaches to Rondônia's development until the year 2020. The Bank has made it clear that all future loans to the State will depend on the ability of the State to adopt more sustainable and consensual approaches. It goes beyond PLANAFLORO in trying to broaden the participatory approach so as to include all levels of government: the legislature, the judiciary, and municipal governments. PLANAFLORO, which was been extended for another two years, has undergone major modifications.[17] While, according to the World Bank, the original objectives of the Project remain unchanged, the structure and management systems have been simplified. The overall approach is to ensure that civil society is involved in project implementation by the inclusion of representative NGOs in the management structure of the project. The project has been divided into two main components: an environmental component, which is centrally administered, responsible for environmental protection schemes, indigenous health care, and zoning; and a development component, which like other social investment funds is to be demand-driven, by which is meant that projects will be proposed and implemented by local communities to meet their needs. The undisbursed Project funds, which amounted to $115 million, have been reallocated between the two. A grant of $18 million has been earmarked for the projects to support community initiatives (Programas de Apoio a Iniciativas Comunitarias — PAICs).

Both Bank management and the NGO Forum believe that communities surrounding protected areas, many of which lack basic amenities, should receive some direct benefit from the project. This in turn should increase public support for its wider goals: respect for State zoning laws and the sustainable management of natural resources. The PAICs offer an interesting challenge to Rondônia's tradition of political patronage. But the PAIC has had forerunners in Rondônia. As a result of NGO complaints about the lack of progress in meeting the needs of poor indigenous and farming communities, there have been various attempts to run micro-projects, none of which has been particularly successful. Local communities were often unaware of the existence of the projects, since they had not participated in their preparation. Oxfam is concerned about the compressed time-scale (12 months) and the large sums of money available, which may lead to the sacrifice of quality in order to meet arbitrary project deadlines. There is a real anxiety that community participation will be seen as little more than a bureaucratic hurdle to be overcome in order to access funds.

The World Bank acknowledges that risks remain. Zoning has placed more than half of the State's territory theoretically off-limits to developers. Those who derive few direct benefits from the project may oppose it. Weaknesses in local institutions cannot easily be addressed, and improvements will take time. The Bank seems to be clearer that its objective is to help to forge a durable constituency in Rondônia which favours sustainable development and is willing to forgo short-term profits that may accrue from predatory use of resources.[18]

EU reforms

As for the European Union, after the problems encountered in Uganda there is some recognition that the Kibale Forest project could have had a much greater impact if it had adopted a more flexible approach and supervision had been improved. The EU accepts that the application of OECD guidelines on resettlement is essential in all such interventions. A decision was taken in 1996 — before the results of an evaluation were ready — to extend the Forest Rehabilitation Programme in Uganda. While the Commission has said that it will try to promote a more sustainable management model and give greater emphasis to participatory processes, Oxfam is not aware of any special training being provided to help to alter the approach of the Forest Department.[19] The EU, however, has withdrawn from a National Parks Project in Southern Ethiopia as a result of concerns about the harmful effects of the proposed exclusion of nomadic pastoralists from their traditional, seasonal grazing lands. In its guidelines for the negotiation of a new co-operation agreement with ACP countries, to replace the current Lomé Convention when it expires in the year 2000, the Commission is pledged to integrate a gender-sensitive approach into all its activities (macro-economic and sectoral project-assistance) and to reduce disparities between men and women. It will also integrate the principles of the Earth Summit by adopting practices conducive to economically, socially and environmentally sustainable development. The EU also recognises that the new development agenda is 'one geared not only to meeting basic needs but to guaranteeing human rights in the political, social and cultural spheres'. For this reason the EU proposes to increase its support for the organisation of civil society and to encourage the introduction of transparent processes for consultation and dialogue.[20]

Participation and the private sector

It is more than a little ironic that, just as some consensus has been reached about the most effective way of promoting development, levels of official aid have started to decline. In 1995, DAC aid amounted to $58,800 million, or 0.27 per cent of GNP, which at the time was the lowest level ever recorded. The real-terms cut in aid compared with the previous year was 9 per cent. In 1996, aid fell yet again to $55,100 million, or 4.2 per cent in real terms, reaching another new low at 0.25 per cent of GNP. Since the Earth Summit in 1992, when developed countries reaffirmed their commitment to the UN target of 0.7 per cent of GNP, aid has fallen by almost 17 per cent in real terms. The world's largest donor, Japan, has announced cuts in its aid from 1998 onwards.[21]

One part of the governance debate, about aid mismanagement, corruption, and waste, has dominated debates in the US Congress; for the foreseeable future the universal engine of development is to be market-led growth. Foreign direct investment (FDI) is supposed increasingly to assume the leading role in efforts to stimulate economic growth in the world's poorest countries. Figures for 1996 show that private flows to developing countries rose by $80,000 million to $234,000 million. In 1988 private flows to developing countries were three-quarters the volume of aid, but they are now four times larger.[23] But the Least Developed Countries attracted throughout the 1990–95 period on average $1.1 billion of FDI inflows, which corresponds to about one half of one per cent of global FDI flows. Poor countries with stagnant economies, inadequate infrastructure, and limited capacity will not suddenly begin attracting private investment. However, organisations like the British government's Commonwealth Development Corporation (CDC) have a specific mandate to assist overseas countries in the development of their economies by promoting private-sector investment.[23] The CDC, recognising that private-capital flows to developing countries are increasing, but in an uneven manner, has sought to redress the balance by focusing on sub-Saharan Africa and South Asia. The CDC is supposed to invest in businesses that are commercially viable and economically sound, and which meet international social and environmental standards.[24] However, the CDC, like its international counterparts, the International Finance Corporation (IFC) and the European Investment Bank, is insufficiently accountable to the public. All documents related to their investments remain confidential, even after a loan has been approved. While it is understandable that these bodies should wish to restrict public access to confidential business information, as the Hair Report into IFC's support for the Pangue Dam in Chile concluded, social and environmental components which represent 'legitimate, "public's right to know" issues' should be disclosed as a matter of routine. Without such information, the public is effectively denied any means of evaluating the success of these loans in meeting their social and environmental objectives, or of ensuring their continued implementation.

The response of private-sector companies to NGO pressure has been mixed. Some, like the Chilean power company ENDESA, which was under threat of being declared in default of the IFC financing agreement over the Pangue dam, paid off its debt obligations to the IFC rather than comply with the recommendations of the Hair Report. But failure to co-operate has its costs. In 1995 the Overseas Private Investment Corporation (OPIC — a US government political-risk insurance agency) suspended insurance from Freeport/RTZ's Grasberg copper-gold mine after NGOs produced evidence that the mining company was dumping toxic waste into the rivers of Irian Jaya (West Papua in Indonesia). But there are signs that some of the leading multinational companies are seeking to change their image and to show NGOs and the wider public that they are taking their environmental and ethical responsibilities seriously.

As traditional sources of funding for development begin to dry up, NGOs have been concerned to ensure that private-sector investors should learn from the experience of official aid institutions. During the

1990s, the view of corporations as businesses with no social or moral responsibility has been increasingly challenged, not least by enlightened business leaders. Their mandate is being seen to extend beyond the maximisation of short-term returns for their shareholders to addressing the concerns of a wider group of stakeholders, including consumers and local communities. Corporate responsibility and governance have become major issues as a result of consumer pressure, concern about employee motivation, and media exposures of corporate malpractice. At least some of the 39,000 transnational corporations and their 270,00 foreign affiliates (whose combined holdings are worth over $42.7 trillion) are recognising that mission statements and guidelines are only as good as their implementation.[25] Social accounting, risk assessments that incorporate political and environmental dimensions, and greater public reporting by companies are extending the remit of corporate governance. Hopes for ethically sound and socially just economic growth will increasingly depend on the acceptance by the private sector of international standards of accountable development.

7 **Lessons learned — and benchmarks for accountable development**

This study of major development programmes in Brazil, India, and Uganda has yielded some general lessons about the need for participatory, locally accountable aid programmes, and some lessons in how to implement them. These learning-points are summarised below.

- It is crucially important to foster partnerships between donors and different levels of government, and between the authorities and civil society.

- It is vital to conduct participatory poverty assessments, social assessments, and stakeholder analyses as the first steps in any intervention. These findings should then inform policy, shape priorities, and determine appropriate participatory mechanisms.

- With indigenous, tribal, or ethnically distinct populations, culturally appropriate plans should be based on a consideration of the options preferred by the beneficiaries or affected groups.

- It is necessary to prioritise preliminary training, for example in budgeting and other technical matters, to enable local people to participate effectively.

- The value of a communications strategy using local media to mobilise people should not be under-estimated.

- There is a need for agreed and properly financed participatory monitoring systems.

- Data collected by monitoring systems, including detailed statistics by geographical areas, should be used and disseminated as a means of encouraging greater local mobilisation, to fine-tune institutional planning, and to correct problems as they arise.

- It is important to build in incentives such as public recognition for achievements by local authorities and communities: there is a need for short-term gains if people's initial enthusiasm is not to be dissipated.

- Effective mechanisms for conflict resolution and mediation are essential: they must be able to respond promptly to *bona fide* concerns and complaints from affected people, through providing redress and compensation.

- Local NGOs can be overstretched. As institutionalised power-sharing becomes routine, local representatives may become unwilling to devote the time needed to make participation work. Unless strategies are in place to help overcome this, the absence of democratic scrutiny may enable local elites once again to reassert themselves and capture project benefits.

- Active community participation in project selection and implementation is a necessary but far from sufficient means of alleviating poverty.

- Merely increasing the flow of funds to local authorities, without changing the institutional structures or improving transparency, may simply reinforce material inequalities and social exclusion.

- In many areas an incremental, selective, and sequential approach which strengthens local administrative capacities will be more effective than wholesale, immediate decentralisation.

- No amount of participation will overcome weak project management or a hostile external environment.

- Partnership is the logical end-goal of participatory efforts. A government's willingness to operate in partnership with civil society should be a major determinant in decisions made by the international community about the level of resources to invest in that country.

Specific lessons for natural-resource management projects

- Unless environmental issues are incorporated into long-term development plans, there is a danger of their becoming 'enclave' projects. For interventions to be successful, there has to be consistency between forest policy and those of other related sectors.

- Forestry projects cannot be concerned with planting and protecting trees. Projects which are aimed solely at forests or the conservation of other areas of biodiversity and which ignore the interests of people are unlikely to be sustainable.

- Traditional methods of controlling and managing large areas of government-protected forests and parks through exclusion and policing are simply not viable. Participatory models, which provide for the joint management of assets with local communities are likely to be much more successful. However, these need to be backed up with legislation which both safeguards local people's entitlements to land and other resources and protects the environment from unsustainable exploitation.

- Benefit-sharing systems need to be carefully worked out to ensure that proceeds are equitably distributed between and within villages or different user-groups.

- Poor, resource-dependent people who are likely to suffer a (short-term) reduction in their access to key resources (such as grazing land or fuel) will need to be compensated or provided with alternatives immediately.

- While it may at times be necessary to remove encroachers from protected areas, this must always be carried out within the framework of the law and international human-rights standards. Distinction must be made between short-term, opportunistic encroachers and longer-term settlers or those who have or may have acquired customary rights to land and other natural resources.

Benchmarks for accountable development

In May 1997 the incoming Labour government in the UK promised to ensure that environmental standards and respect for human rights would be at the centre of its foreign policy. Britain's Department for International Development has also clearly indicated in the Government's White Paper its intention of adopting a rights-based approach to development.[1] The EU's policy guidelines for future co-operation with African, Caribbean, and Pacific countries — once the current Lomé Convention expires in the year 2000 — also seek to promote a development model that guarantees human rights and social progress.[2] But there is some confusion about what exactly a rights-based approach would entail and how it might be put into practice. From Oxfam's experience and an analysis of the cases reported in this study, some general guidelines have emerged. Such an approach requires sensitivity to local situations, so that any aid interventions or investments do not do more harm than good. Development interventions should never leave poor people with reduced possibilities for sustaining themselves and their families. The access of poor people to goods, services, or use and control of natural resources should not be diminished without adequate and appropriate compensation. In Oxfam's view, a rights-based approach needs to incorporate six principles of action derived from acknowledged human-rights standards. These principles should be respected by donors — governments, international financial institutions, NGOs, and private companies. They provide clear benchmarks for evaluating accountable development. The core principles are *due diligence; non-discrimination; advisability; participation; accountability;* and *redress.*

Due diligence: Donors or private agents have an obligation to exercise due care before undertaking a project or investment operation. This means, among other things, examining and taking into account the political, social, and environmental context; consulting widely with representatives of civil society (not just with governments); and ensuring that donors are aware of the most recent human-rights reports on the public record.

Non-discrimination: This is a basic tenet of all international human-rights law. Donors have an obligation to ensure that development initiatives do not increase divisions in a recipient country, for example between ethnic groups, or otherwise contribute to perpetuating discriminatory practices. The impacts of interventions on women and young girls must always be carefully assessed and potential problems addressed in the design of development or private investment programmes.

Advisability: Multilateral agencies, donors, or other private agents should respect the provision of the International Covenant on Economic, Social and Cultural Rights, which emphasises the need to ensure that development co-operation activities enhance the ability of recipient governments to promote economic and social rights, including the rights to an adequate standard of living, and to access to education, and the best possible level of health care. Development interventions that lead to a

147

deterioration of these standards can be deemed 'inadvisable' and in violation of the spirit of international human-rights law.

Participation: International human-rights standards have long recognised the right of individuals and communities to be involved in the formulation and implementation of policies, programmes, budgets, legislation, and other activities (Article 25a of the International Covenant on Civil and Political Rights, ICCPR). The right to participation is clearly connected to civil and political rights, but is specifically applicable to the realisation of Economic, Social and Cultural Rights (Paragraph 11 of the Limburg Principles — which were developed at an experts' meeting in 1987). Article 2 (I) of the Declaration on the Right to Development states that 'the human person is the central subject of development and should be the active participant and beneficiary of the right to development'. Principle 10 of the Rio Declaration recognises that environmental issues are best handled with the participation of all concerned citizens. It is recognised that effective participation requires access to information about development and environmental initiatives held by public authorities or donors or even private companies.

Accountability: Donors, private companies, and governments have a duty to accept responsibility for their actions. This requires them to be transparent in their undertakings and honest in the presentation of operations to civil society and stakeholders. It means that they must take particular care to consult with local communities and to keep them informed during implementation of specific projects and programmes. It also requires them to be prepared to submit their operations to independent scrutiny and oversight. Where changes have to be made to programmes or operations, they should be based, as far as possible, on consensus. However, additional measures may have to be taken to protect the rights and interests of vulnerable groups. If problems arise, it is unacceptable for donors and private companies to simply withdraw from engagement.

Redress: Principle 10 of the Rio Declaration calls on governments to provide effective access to judicial and administrative proceedings, including redress and remedy. This should apply also to donors and private-sector actors. Whereas local people's access to information has improved over the past few years, there has been almost no progress in ensuring effective remedies. International environmental law, with its emphasis on building consensus and improving policy, has failed to promote procedures to protect the rights of individual or communities.

Most of the multilateral agencies have followed the World Bank's example and set up complaints mechanisms, but obtaining effective and timely remedial action when development initiatives cause harm to local people is still a protracted and thankless process. With the privatisation of development, it is even more urgent for private companies to ensure that credible dispute-settlement mechanisms are put in place at the outset of their operations. Donors and companies need to ensure that there is a fair process for adjudicating legitimate claims, given the difficulties — political, financial and cultural — that confront poor communities when they try to gain access to the courts.

Appendix

NGOs and participation: the benefits of forest protection in Orissa

This report is mainly concerned with officially sponsored natural-resource management — by the World Bank, the British government's bilateral aid agency, DFID (formerly ODA), and the European Union. The role of the non-government organisations is examined only in so far as they are participating in officially conceived programmes. Oxfam, in common with many other NGOs, has, of course, supported smaller-scale projects, designed to improve people's awareness of the need for sensitive management of the natural environment and to improve their access to and control over natural resources. From disseminating water-harvesting techniques and supporting small-scale local initiatives to protect genetic resources — the essential underpinning of sustainable agricultural systems — Oxfam has also been involved in attempts to promote community forest-conservation projects, mainly in Brazil and India.[1]

Since 1983, Oxfam has been working in Orissa State in India, where 44 per cent of the population live below the poverty line (compared with 29 per cent for India as a whole).[2] Oxfam's work in Orissa has been substantially financed by the British government.[3] The BOJBP project — Friends of the Trees and Living Beings — has been supported by Oxfam by means of block grants from DFID. The purpose of the project is to promote forest-conservation work by villagers and to raise awareness of environmental issues. BOJBP started work in the context of severe degradation of village forests. It gradually spread out from a core of 22 villages committed to protection, through the work of volunteers who journeyed around the countryside, spreading the word to other villages. BOJBP now works with 324 villages, but it is estimated that more than 2,500 villages are involved in the protection of forests in Orissa.[4] A recent evaluation of this project suggests that smaller-scale projects have not necessarily been more successful in handling some of the complex problems confronted by their larger official counterparts: how to ensure the participation of the poorest and the equitable distribution of benefits. The evaluation report found that, not surprisingly, people were experiencing more benefits from protected forests than from plantations. Because of the existing rootstock and the species diversity of the natural forest areas, benefits were available within a much shorter time. Plantation benefits were confined to leaf litter and, after a time, limited grazing, with the main benefit — the harvesting of wood for construction and firewood purposes — being years into the future. But looking at the equity aspects of forest protection from a broader perspective across whole districts, the study noted that there were large-scale processes causing inequalities between villages. Geography inevitably creates inequalities. Some villages have to share a large forest area with many other villages; some have much smaller areas for the exclusive use of themselves and/or a few other villages; and some are not adjacent to forests at all. Different rates of forest degradation and different degrees of awareness and concern have prompted some villages to take action and to exercise protective control over some forest much earlier than others. The study was critical of BOJBP (and by extension Oxfam) for not having taken any specific action to address these wider issues of equity, through (for example) lobbying government to suggest ways in which such disputes might be mediated in the future.

Evidence from village visits suggested that some smaller villages were concerned about being disadvantaged by the larger villages with whom they share access to a forest area. The study recognised that a newly created body representing all the villages associated with BOJBP might help to mediate in conflicts between member villages. Nevertheless the study registered concern about the fact that 'there are no guarantees, beyond tradition, that the interests of the poorest in a village will be represented' in village committees. It warned that committees representing aggregates of villages or sub-villages were likely simply to replicate the power relationships that already exist between the component villages.

The management rules, which have the potential both to help and harm the poorest in a village, are decided by each village. In some villages even the collection of twigs is forbidden, whereas in others headloading is allowed, with a small fee being charged per load. Given that the constitution of village committees does not automatically guarantee a voice for the poor, the evaluation team believed that BOJBP had an obligation at least to identify the rules that were in practice and to promote those rules which would seem to protect the interests of the poorest. Clearly, management rules have to be appropriate to local conditions, and are best decided locally. But there need to be guidelines. In a *harijan* ('untouchable') village, 75 per cent of households are partially dependent on firewood sales. Sometimes wood cutting has been displaced to more distant unprotected forests. Wood-cutting families are paying the costs of protection, in increased walking distances, or in harassment and fines. The project was criticised for failing to address the issue of alternative livelihoods. Solutions such as establishing a firewood plantation to meet the needs of the wood-cutters were rejected in some areas, because village committees were reluctant to allocate any special usage rights in forest areas to particular groups, for fear of opening up the possibility of others making special private claims on 'common' land.

But the greatest concern was voiced about the lack of an agreed benefit-sharing system. The report commented that 'The equity issues concerned with current management of the forests pale into insignificance when compared to the impending problems of the future. The forests and plantations are maturing assets, increasing in value and visibility every day. None of the villages contacted had established any long term management plans, especially for the allocation of benefits from plantations.' While the study admits that this might be an unreasonable expectation, it goes on to stress how current decisions, such as to plant trees over a whole area, rather than on a rotational basis, section by section, have implications for the villages concerned to take continuing yield from the land. This in turn will affect the management of claims for benefits, with one-off distributions being more problematic.

The study commended the fact that, as a result of the project, 'all women, whether better-off castes or poorer Harijan women' recognised the importance of forest protection. Villagers were anxious to indicate improvements to their quality of life, such as the re-emergence of water in what had been dried-up streams; streams flowing for longer periods of the year; wells recharging and remaining full for a longer period; and the improved fertility of fields adjacent to forested areas.

Organised forest protection by village forest-protection committees is not confined to BOJBP's area, but is prevalent in many parts of Orissa and other parts of India. But the study warns:

What is striking about many of these other efforts, however, is their early descent into chaos and a kind of manic slaughter of trees. The pattern appears to be one whereby perception of the problems caused by deforestation leads to the organisation of forest protection; after a period of time, usually less than 10 years, fears about equity of distribution of the proceeds of any logging or the fear of raids by outsiders, coupled with the need for timber, lead to the breaking of ranks, after which a free for all ensues as everyone tries to ensure that they get their share, and forests are frequently reduced to the state they were in before the latest bout of forest protection.[5]

However, the report concedes that the value of BOJBP's moral force lies in the relatively long time-span over which forest-protection work has flourished in the project's sphere of influence. BOJBP started formally in 1982, but it had its origins in the mid-1970s. The report points out that, whereas some of the benefits of forest protection — increased rainfall over villages, reduced erosion, consequently reduced siltation of village tanks, increased shade — accrue equally to all villages, others — fruit, medicinal products, useful bark, and most importantly a potentially substantial revenue from the harvest of valuable timber — will accrue only to those villages which have substantial natural forest which has been allowed to regenerate, and not to those which are protecting primarily monoculture plantations.

A key conclusion of the evaluation report is that, whatever the nature of the potential benefits, some of them can be realised only within a favourable legal and institutional context. Such a context will be one in which villagers undertaking forest protection can feel secure in their entitlement to these benefits. This applies particularly to the revenue from any harvest of timber. Finally the evaluation set out its six recommendations for a strategy of sustainable forest protection, which BOJBP and Oxfam are now trying to implement:

- to persuade the Forest Department to shift from monoculture plantations to the plantation of indigenous species, in consultation with local people;

- to provide some education for villagers in the techniques of scientific forest management;

- to formalise the potential rights made available to forest-protecting villages;

- to establish a framework for dividing the proceeds of any timber harvest equitably within villages, which will be acceptable to all (or at least to a substantial majority);

- to include, as part of such a framework, some provision for use of wood for those villagers, such as potters, who have identifiably distinct needs;

- to develop a mediation body whose authority will be accepted at least by villages within the BOJBP area in relation to disputes between villages over access to forests.

Notes

Chapter 1

1 Article 25a of the International Covenant on Civil and Political Rights, ICCPR, and Paragraph 11 of the Limburg Principles — which were developed at an experts' meeting in 1987.

2 Moeen A. Qureshi, Senior Vice President, Operations: 'Popular Participation and the World Bank' (speaking at the International Development Conference, 'From Cold War to Co-operation: Dynamics of a New World Order', January 1991).

3 DAC High-Level Meeting, Paris, December 1990, session on Participatory Development.

4 World Bank: *Sub-Saharan Africa: From Crisis to Sustainable Growth*, Washington: World Bank, 1989.

5 'Good Government and the Aid Programme', speech by Baroness Chalker to Chatham House, 26 June 1991.

6 'Managing Development: The Governance Dimension', a Discussion Paper, August 1991, Washington: World Bank.

7 World Bank: *World Development Report*, 1997, Washington: World Bank, 1997.

8 DAC Expert Group on Aid Evaluation: *Evaluation of Programs Promoting Participatory Development and Good Governance*, Synthesis Report, Paris: OECD, 1997.

9 World Bank: *The World Bank and Participation*, Washington: World Bank, September 1994.

10 *The Bank's World*, April 1991, 'Participatory Development: A New Imperative for our Times'.

11 World Bank: *Participation Sourcebook*, Washington: World Bank, 1996.

12 The British bilateral aid agency was known until 1997 as the Overseas Development Administration (ODA), and operated as part of the Foreign and Commonwealth Office. Now called the Department For International Development (DFID), it is a separate

Ministry. 'ODA' is used in this text to describe British aid when dealing with projects, policies, and programmes approved before May 1997.

13 'Social Development Handbook — A Guide to Social Issues in ODA Projects and Programmes', Overseas Development Administration, London, 1993.

14 'Note on Enhancing Stakeholder Participation in Aid Activities', ODA, April 1995.

15 J. H. Michel: *Development Co-operation, DAC 1995 Report*, Paris: OECD, 1996.

16 Jonathan Fox and Josefina Aranda: *Decentralization and Rural Development in Mexico: Community Participation in Oaxaca's Municipal Funds Programme*, 1996, Monograph Series, 42, Center for US–Mexican Studies, University of California, San Diego.

17 UNDP: *Human Development Report*, United Nations Development Programme, New York: Oxford University Press, 1996.

18 Norwegian Ministry for Foreign Affairs 'Approach Paper on Decentralization', February 1997. See DAC Expert Group on Aid Evaluation, *Evaluation of Programmes Promoting Participatory Development and Good Governance*, Synthesis Report, Paris: OECD, 1997.

19 Operations Evaluation Department: *Effectiveness of Environmental Assessments and National Environmental Action Plans: A Process Study*, Washington: OED, World Bank, 28 June 1996.

20 See 'Institutional Appraisal and Development Methodology Programme Phase One', April 1995, evaluation report drawn up on behalf of the Commission of the European Communities; and 'Assessment of WID/Gender policies of the Community and its member states and of their implementation by the different administrations', 1/10/94; and 'Inventory of Environment and Tropical Forests Programmes — Final Report March 1996'; and 'Evaluation of EU Aid to ACP Countries Managed by the Commission' Phase 1, Final Report, July 1997.

21 DAC Review of European Community Aid OECD, Paris 1996.

22 The EU's aid programme consists of several components which are managed and financed differently. One is directed at 70 African, Caribbean, and Pacific (ACP) States under a programme governed by the Lomé Convention and financed mainly through the European Development Fund (EDF).

23 ADE, 'Evaluation of EU Aid to ACP Countries Managed by the Commission: Phase 1 Report'.

24 Wilfried Martens, MEP, Draft Report to the European Parliament on the Future of Lomé, p.23.

25 'Openness in the Community, Annex III: Openness and Transparency as They Relate to the General Public', Official Journal of the European Communities, No. C166/4,17 June 1993.

26 'Culture shock for Whitehall', *The Guardian*, 12 December.

27 Quoted in *Non-Governmental Organisations — Performance and Accountability*, edited by Michael Edwards and David Hulme, London: Earthscan, 1995.

28 Nancy Alexander and Charles Abugre: 'NGOs and the International Monetary and Financial System', October 1996 — a paper prepared for the Technical Group of the Intergovernmental Group of Twenty Four on International Monetary Affairs.

29 *Reality of Aid*, edited by Judith Randell and Tony German, ICVA and Eurostep, London: Earthscan, 1996.

30 Lawyers Committee for Human Rights: 'The World Bank, NGOs and Freedom of Association', New York, November 1997.

31 *Searching for Impact and Methods: NGO Evaluation and Synthesis Study*, a report prepared for the OECD/DAC Expert Group on Evaluation, May 1997, by Sten-Erik Kruse *et al.*

32 The DAC report singled out the Oxfam UK/I project in Wajir, north-east Kenya, as one of the best examples of participatory evaluation.

Chapter 2

1 See IBRD, *Integrated Development of the Northwest Frontier*, Washington DC: International Bank for Reconstruction and Development (World Bank), Latin American and Caribbean Regional Office, 1981.

2 According to the World Bank, recent analysis of migration data shows that the peak of the migration occurred in 1981, before the paving of the BR 364 was completed (letter to Oxfam from Gobind Nankani, Director of the Brazil Country Management Unit, 19 September 1997). However, according to the OED 1992 report, the population in the project-affected areas rose from an estimated 620,000 in 1982 to 1.6 million in 1988 (see OED, 'World Bank Approaches to the Environment in Brazil', vol. 5: 'The POLONOROESTE Program', 1992).

3 There were attempts by the Bank to protect Indigenous Areas: in 1983 and 1984, for example, squatters were removed from the Sete

de Setembro and Igarape Lourdes Indian Reserves at the direct behest of the World Bank supervision team.

4   Speech to the Governors, Annual Meetings of the World Bank/IMF, Washington 1987.

5   In 1997 the MST calculated that over 100,000 people had been informally settled after occupying large estates throughout Brazil and were awaiting a decision by the Brazilian government to recognise their claims.

6   The Brazilian Government's Decree 2.550 and Medida Provisoria (Emergency Measure) No. 1.577, which modify Agrarian Law No 8.629/93, Folha de São Paulo, 13 June 1997.

7   Alison Sutton, *Slavery in Brazil: A Link in the Chain of Modernisation, The Case of Brazil*, No 7 in Anti-Slavery International Human Rights Series, Anti-Slavery Society, London, 1994.

8   OD 4.20 (1991) emphasises the need to ensure that indigenous people are not adversely affected by Bank projects and that the social and economic benefits they receive are in harmony with their cultural preferences. Bank staff also must ensure the informed participation of indigenous people in the preparation, design, and implementation of projects.

9   Field Report, 'Population and Land Use and Malaria on the Amazon Frontier: the Case of Machadinho d'Oeste, Rondônia, Brazil', prepared for the Centro de Desenvolvimento e Planejamento Regional — CEDPLAR, Universidade Federal de Minas Gerais, March 1996.

10 World Bank, 'The World Bank, the environment and development', Washington: *World Bank News*, May 1992.

11 Inspection Panel, 'Report on Additional Review, 12 December 1995', Inspection Panel, World Bank.

12 World Bank, 'Staff Appraisal Report, Rondônia Natural Resource Management Project', 27 February 1992.

13 Bruce Rich, *Mortgaging the Earth*, Boston: Beacon Press, 1994.

14 Letter signed by 11 NGOs, dated 12 May 1992, to Luiz Coirolo, Task Manager, World Bank.

15 Letter to Oxfam signed by Demetrios Papageorgiou, Acting Director Country Department 1 Latin America and the Caribbean Regional Office, 6 July 1992.

16 Staff Appraisal Report, Rondônia Natural Resource Management Project, 27 February 1992.

17 All lands in Rondônia are legally divided into six distinct categories: **Zone 1** is the most densely populated part of Rondônia, where official colonisation projects have been concentrated. The soil quality is generally good for cultivation. **Zone 2** is less densely populated, with moderate to poor soil quality, and there has been unofficial settlement interspersed with cattle ranching. **Zone 3** is in the northern part of Rondônia, along the flooded margins of the Mamore, Madeira, and Machado rivers, where small settled populations make their livelihoods from sustainable agricultural systems, fishing, and non-wood forest extraction activities. **Zone 4** includes areas which have potential for sustainable extractive non-wood production (e.g. rubber-tapping, Brazil-nut collection, perfumes, etc). **Zone 5** is reserved for sustainable forest management, with selective logging and replacement/enrichment of exploited species. **Zone 6** includes the most fragile ecosystems without potential for sustainable use. It also covers the Amerindian and biological reserves and national forests. In this zone, critical conservation units and reserves need to be demarcated and protected, and forest cover totally maintained.

18 Agro-forestry research, rural extension, credit, and input supply would be concentrated in Zone 1, where the focus would be on intensification of farming systems. Forest cover would be maintained on all steep slopes and poorer soils. In Zone 2, the project would assist established farming communities only; the expansion of cattle ranching would be halted by the government. Forest management and improved extraction of non-wood forest products would be concentrated in Zones 3, 4, and 5. Project activities for Zone 6 would be to manage and protect conservation units and Indian reserves.

19 World Bank Press Backgrounder on PLANAFLORO, September 1996.

20 The original field work was undertaken in May and June 1994 by a three-person team headed by Mario Menezes, an agronomist and specialist in extractive reserves, working with Dr Marcio Silva, an anthropologist at UNICAMP, São Paulo State, and Patricia Feeney, of Oxfam's Policy Department. Their report for Oxfam was entitled 'Avaliação de Agropecuário no Plano — Agropecuário e Florestal de Rondônia' (Mario Menezes, Brazil, June 1994). Additional interviews and field visits were carried out by the Project's co-ordinator, Patricia Feeney. Brent Millikan, a PhD candidate from the University of California, Berkeley, who is based in Rondônia

and an adviser to the NGO Forum, worked as a consultant for Oxfam, providing invaluable research on POLONOROESTE, and the impact of Public Policies in Rondônia. In 1996 Oxfam commissioned Horacio Martins de Carvalho, a consultant agronomist, to evaluate the impact of the Forum's activities; his report for Oxfam Recife (October 1996) was entitled 'Resgate Histórico e Avaliação do Forum das Organizações Não Governamentais e Movimentos Sociais que Atuam em Rondônia'.

21 In 1997, the Federal Prosecutor's Office in Rondônia found after an investigation that land expropriations by INCRA-Rondônia had been systematically overvalued for several years. The Brazilian media reported these findings widely in late 1996/97 after the assassination in São Paulo of Fernando Ibere, a leading figure implicated in the scandal.

22 Patricia Feeney, 'From POLONOROESTE to PLANAFLORO: Has the World Bank Learnt its Lesson?', Policy Department Briefing Paper, Oxfam UK/Ireland, 1994.

23 Amnesty International, *Brazil Briefing*, London: Amnesty International Publications, 1988 and *Rural Violence in Brazil*, Washington: An Americas Watch Report, 1991.

24 Section 2.12 (a) of the Project Agreement and Section 6.01 (b) of the Loan Agreement.

25 Under Brazilian law, peasants who have occupied and cultivated land for over a year and a day acquire certain rights of tenure. With these rights of 'posse' — possession — they have become known as 'posseiros'. They are entitled to apply for ownership of the land if they have occupied and cultivated it uncontested for five years.

26 Brent Millikan, Field Report: 'Population and Land Use and Malaria on the Amazon Frontier', March 1996

27 'Governo muda a lei e quer dar um basta a invasões', Folha de São Paulo, 13 June 1997.

28 Interview with the environmental NGO, Ecoporé.

29 The Forum's concerns would appear to have been well founded. On 11 June 1996 a legal injunction was issued, requiring Oswaldo Piana Filho, the former Governor, William José Cury (the former Secretary of Planning), and José Lacerda de Mello (the former Secretary of PLANAFLORO) to return to the public treasury money that had formed part of the World Bank loan but which had not been transmitted to the implementing agencies.

30 Sr Alfredo Ruiz, comunidade de Sto Antonio, Município de Pimenta Bueno.
31 'Mudou o prato mas a comida é a mesma. O governo não usa dinheiro para criar reserva, só fazenda' (Ze Maria, President of OSR).
32 Section 2.11 of the Project Agreement.
33 This section, in particular the views of the project's beneficiaries, draws on the interim report of Oxfam's Evaluation of Participation in PLANAFLORO: 'Avaliação de Participação no Plano Agropecuário e Florestal de Rondônia', Mario Menezes, Brazil June 1994.
34 Inspection Panel, 'Request for Inspection, Brazil: Rondônia Natural Resource Management Project (Loan 3444-BR), Report Review of Progress in Implementation', World Bank, Washington March 26 1997.

Chapter 3

1   UNDP: *Human Development Report*, New York: Oxford University Press, 1997.
2   Many international instruments, declarations and analyses place great emphasis on the participation of women in public life and have set a framework of international standards of equality. These include the Universal Declaration of Human Rights, the International Covenant on Civil and Political Rights, paragraph 13 of the Beijing Declaration and Platform for Action, general recommendations 5 and 8 under the Convention, general comment 25 adopted by the Human Rights Committee, the recommendation adopted by the Council of the European Union on balanced participation of women and men in the decision-making process, and the European Commission's 'How to Create a Gender Balance in Political Decision Making'.
3   S. Kulkarni, 'Towards a social forestry policy', *Economic and Political Weekly*, 8(6) February 1983.
4   Bina Agarwal, *Gender, Environment and Poverty Interlinks in Rural India*, United Nations Research Institute for Social Development Discussion Paper, Geneva, UNRISD, April 1995.
5   Under common-property regimes the right to exploit common-pool resources is held by a defined set of people in conjunction with one another, as opposed to common-pool resources, which are regarded as being 'open access'.
6   But ODA also hoped that support for social forestry in Karnataka would offset criticism of its funding of another project, the Mysore

Paper Mills Forestry Project, in which public lands were being planted with monoculture eucalyptus.

7   In Reserve Forests, government lands which are for the most part closed to local use; 19 per cent are degraded. In protected forest areas, known as *soppinabettas*, which are exclusively for private use, 81 per cent of the land is degraded. In Minor Forests, which are areas set aside for local use to supply non-timber forest products or firewood, 95 per cent is degraded.

8   Appiko is the Kannada synonym for Chipko (hugging the trees). Chipko is a grassroots struggle in the Himalayas in which villagers hugged trees to save them from felling, after deforestation and soil erosion threatened their survival.

9   *Arecanut* is a horticultural crop grown as a cash crop in moderately sized private plantations (1-2 ha). The *Arecanut* gardeners are mainly higher-caste (Havak Brahmins) farmers. *Soppinabetta* lands are forest lands under private tenure allocated to older *areca* gardeners to provide their requirements for forest produce.

10 Catherine Locke, 'Planning for the Participation of Vulnerable Groups in Communal Management of Forest Resources: The Case of the Western Ghats Forestry Project', a thesis submitted for the Degree of Doctor of Philosophy, Centre for Development Studies, University of Wales, June 1995.

11 N.C. Saxena, Madhu Sarin, R.V. Singh, Tushaar Shah, 'Western Ghats Forestry Project: Independent Study of Implementation Experience in Kanara Circle', May 1997.

12 Ibid.

13 Zone 1: ecologically important areas; Zone 2: main forest zone without forest dwellers; Zone 3: main forest zone with pockets of settlements; Zone 4: edge of forest reserve near settlements; Zone 5: outside forest near settlements.

14 Oxfam 'Report of the Mid-Term Review of Oxfam's Parallel NGO Project in the Western Ghats', January 1995.

15 Dr Mariette Correa, 'Evaluation of NTFP Work in Oxfam JFPM Support Project, Uttara Kannada', February 1997, Oxfam India Trust New Delhi.

16 Locke, op. cit.

17 Pandurang Hegde, 'Commercialisation of Tropical Forests of Western Ghats — A Case Study of the Western Ghats Forestry Project', Parisara Sanmrakshana Kendra, Sirsi, Uttara Kannada, December 1995.

18 NGO Network on JFPM, Uttara Kannada, 'A Review of the JFPM Process', February 1995.
19 Saxena *et al*. 1997.
20 S.D. Ashley, Syed Ajmal Pasha, P. Mahale, C.R.C. Hendy, G.R. Hegde, 'A Study of the Role of Livestock in the Livelihoods of Communities in Uttara Kannada', Government of India, Karnataka Forest Department, Overseas Development Administration, December 1993.
21 'The public and private spheres of human activity have always been considered distinct, and have been regulated accordingly. Invariably, women have been assigned to the private or domestic sphere, associated with reproduction and the raising of children, and in all societies these activities have been treated as inferior. By contrast, public life, which is respected and honoured, extends to a broad range of activity outside the private and domestic sphere. Men historically have both dominated public life and exercised power to confine and subordinate women within the private sphere', Implementation of Article 21 of the Convention on the Elimination of All Forms of Discrimination against Women, Draft General Recommendation No. 23 (articles 7 and 8) Article 7 (political and public life), CEDAW/C/1997/II/5 30 May 1997.
22 Profile of Saralgi Village, Mariette Correa, 'Gender and Joint Forest Planning and Management — A research study in Uttara Kannada District, Karnataka', India Development Service, Dharwad, Karnataka, November 1995.
23 Ibid.
24 In Uttara Kannada Circle there are only three women forest guards and one woman forester.
25 Robert Chambers, *Whose Reality Counts?*, Intermediate Technology Publications, London, 1997.
26 Ibid.
27 Independent Review.
28 Locke, op. cit.

Chapter 4

1 Since the Treaty of European Union was agreed in Maastricht in 1992, the term 'European Union' has come into general use to refer to the member states collectively. Legal instruments continue to be adopted by the European Community, since the European Union

has no legal personality. As the Finance Agreement for the Uganda Natural Forest Management and Conservation Project pre-dates the signing of the Maastrict Treaty, the term 'EC' is used for matters that occurred before the Treaty of Union.

2   This tendency of the EU's environment co-operation strategies to ignore social dimensions persists. On 23 October 1997 the European Commission held a public consultation on its draft Europe–Asia Environmental Co-operation Strategy. While the draft strategy pays considerable attention to global environmental problems, there is virtually no mention of the human dimension: issues such as public participation, land rights, and the threats facing the region's indigenous peoples are conspicuous by their absence.

3   BMB: Institutional Development Study — Final Report, Vol. 1 Synthesis April 1996, para 3.4.2 and General Conclusions. A report drawn up on behalf of the European Commission.

4   World Bank, 'Resettlement and Development: The Bankwide Review of Projects Involving Involuntary Resettlement 1986–1993', Environment Department Papers, Paper No. 032, the World Bank, Washington, March 1996.

5   In 1980 the World Bank issued its initial resettlement policy, entitled 'Social Issues Associated with Involuntary Resettlement in Bank-Financed Projects' (OMS 2.33). In 1986 revised guidelines were issued as an Operations Policy Note (OPN 10.08). In 1988, for the first time the World Bank made its resettlement policy public, in Technical Paper No 80, which combined both the earlier policy documents. In 1990 the resettlement policy was revised and reissued as Operational Directive 4.30: Involuntary Resettlement. But in 1997, the policy was weakened when the World Bank 'reformatted' its OD in order to 'clarify some ambiguities'.

6   Development Assistance Committee, 'Guidelines for Aid Agencies on Involuntary Displacement and Resettlement in Development', OECD, Paris, 1991.

7   Evaluation of the EDF-Funded Natural Forest Management and Conservation Project — a Component of the World Bank Forestry Rehabilitation Project, Uganda (1988-1995), Volume 1, LTS International, Edinburgh, July 1996 (hereafter referred to as 'LTS Evaluation Report').

8   Ibid.

9   Ibid., para 3.10.

10 'Resettlement Policy and Institutional Capacity for Resettlement Planning in Uganda', report prepared by Government of Uganda, Office of the Prime Minister, Kampala, March 1995.

11 Ibid., page 16.

12 L. Wily, Mount Elgon Conservation and Development Project. Technical Report 10, September 1993.

13 LTS Evaluation Report, paras 7.15 and 10.15.

14 See note 5.

15 Evaluation of EU Aid to ACP Countries Managed by the Commission, Phase 1, Final Report, July 1997, ADE.

16 See Derek E. Earle: 'Final Report: Chief Technical Adviser of the EC-financed Natural Forest and Management and Conservation Project' (Kampala, November 1992).

17 'All involuntary resettlement should be conceived and executed as development programmes, providing sufficient investment resources and opportunities for resettlers to share in project benefits. Displaced people should be i) enabled to reconstruct a land-based or employment-based productive existence; ii) compensated for their losses at replacement cost; iii) assisted with the move and during the transition period at the relocation site; and iv) assisted in their efforts to improve their former living standards and income earning capacity, and production levels, or at least to restore them.'

18 Tom Barton and Gimono Wamai, 'Equity and Vulnerability: A Situation Analysis of Women, Adolescents and Children in Uganda', Government of Uganda and the Ugandan Council for Children, Kampala, October 1994.

19 'A Report on the Investigations into the Manner in which the Eviction of People from South Kibale Forest Reserve and Game Corridor was Carried Out', Cabinet Committee, Kampala, December 1992.

20 The Kibale Forest Reserve was then under the gazetted authority of the Department of Forestry in the Ministry of Energy, Minerals and Environment Protection. The area was covered by the EC's Natural Forest Management and Conservation Project. The Kibale Game Corridor is gazetted as a game reserve: it is situated between the Queen Elizabeth National Park and the Kibale Forest Reserve. It includes the parish of Mpokya, from which the Mpokya Forest derives its name. The Mpokya Forest is a wooded area of the Game Corridor, but is not a gazetted forest reserve. At the time of the

evictions, about 30,000 people were living in the Game Corridor, which was under the jurisdiction of the Department of Wildlife in the Ministry of Tourism, Wildlife and Antiquities. According to a study by the Land Tenure Center of the University of Wisconsin-Madison, by 1989 the area had ceased functioning as a game corridor in any meaningful sense of the term.

21 On 28 March 1992, the Inspector General of Government warned the District Administrator of Kabarole that the evictions should not go ahead, as there was a risk of human-rights violations. On the evening of 30 March 1992, the letter of the 3rd Deputy Prime Minister in which he called for the suspension of the eviction exercise was read out on the radio.

22 The EC originally insisted to Oxfam that the Kibale expulsions did not involve either the Ugandan Forest Department or project funds. It later amended this to an acknowledgement that EDF funds 'might have been diverted and used in the evictions from the Game Corridor'. The existence of two alternative forest boundaries accounted for much of the ensuing confusion. In July 1993 the Forest Department admitted that nearly 20,000 ecus had been spent at Kibale, mainly on operations to evict settlers. After its December 1993 mission, the EC concluded that evictions were 'not among the tasks presented in any official EC document. The fact that this support has partly been diverted and misused to violently evict people from the area does not mean that this operation was part of the EC-funded project'. In an attempt to distance the EC from the Kibale evictions, the Ugandan government was asked to pay back the sum used (about 20,000 ecus). But the LTS evaluation report notes a major contradiction in the Commission's line of reasoning: if evictions *per se* were outside the Financing Agreement, all funds committed for evictions (not just the Kibale operations) over the period *1988-92* would also need to be repaid. This has not happened (see LTS Evaluation Report, Annex 12).

23 Cabinet Committee Report, December 1992.

24 Testimony of one of the women settlers.

25 Interview with the CGR of Kibale District.

26 Michael M. Cernea, 'Understanding and preventing impoverishment from displacement: reflections on the state of knowledge' in *Understanding Impoverishment, The Consequences of Development-Induced Displacement* (edited by Christopher McDowell),Berg-Hahn Books, Oxford, 1996.

27 LTS Evaluation Report, Annex para 16.9.3.

28 URDT Report.

29 Information Memo to the EDF Committee, 20 October 1993.

30 Oxfam UK and Ireland, Ugandan Rural Development and Training Programme (URDT), and the Bugangaizi Resettlers Association (BRA), 'Submission to the Committee on Economic, Social and Cultural Rights', April 1996.

31 The mission consisted of representatives of the EC, the Ugandan government, Oxfam, and URDT, a Ugandan NGO working in Bugangaizi.

32 LTS Evaluation Report, paras 3.4 –3.7.

33 To put the 300,000 ecu community-development project in perspective, it is worth noting that in 1992/93, when approximately 15,000 people were resettled at Bugangaizi, Oxfam and other NGOs, with support from the British government, provided emergency assistance worth $1.4 million. The government of Uganda provided $0.6 million.

34 Memorandum to the Delegate of the Commission in Uganda dated 10 May 1989 concerning the Six Monthly Report of the Forestry Rehabilitation project.

35 LTS Evaluation Report, para 9.30.

Chapter 5

1 The Panel noted in its report that a review of Aide Memoires from November 1992 up to October 1995 shows how deadlines set for implementation of various tasks were repeatedly unmet. The solution was to agree to another deadline in the next supervision mission's Aide Memoire. In other cases dates for completion of activities were set, but frequently there was no follow-up. For example, one mission concluded that the Amerindian component 'is suffering from an overall lack of implementation', while Indian reserves had been invaded by squatters, miners, and illegal loggers. However, the Bank mission did not establish specific tasks or deadlines to improve monitoring and enforcement. 'The lack of commitment of both parties to such deadlines is evidenced by the fact that they neglected to update the specific deadlines set forth in the loan and project agreements. Indeed, as a result, through these repeated informal extensions their enforcement became increasingly unlikely.'

2   Richard E. Bissell, 'Institutional and Procedural Aspects: Composition and Functions', a paper prepared for an Expert Meeting on the Inspection Panel, held in October 1997 at the Raoul Wallenberg Institute of Human Rights and Humanitarian Law, Lund University, Sweden.

3   Ibrahim Shihata: *The World Bank Inspection Panel* (IBRD/World Bank, Oxford University Press, New York, 1994).

4   Bissell, op. cit.

5   The Lomé Convention determines the principles and instruments of development co-operation between the EC and African, Caribbean and Pacific (ACP) States. It is now under its fourth revision and draws the bulk of its financing from the European Development Fund (EDF).

6   Lomé IV was revised at a meeting in Mauritius on 4 November 1995.

7   EU Commission, 'Policy Guidelines for future EU–ACP relations', October 1997.

8   Lomé Convention Articles 193 and 216(2).

9   Article F1 of the Treaty of Union.

10   Oxfam Policy Department, 'A Profile of European Aid II: Northern Corridor Transport Project. Adverse Social and Environmental Impacts caused by the Rehabilitation of the Westlands-St Austin and Kabete-Limuru roads, Kenya, September 1996.

11   Ref 983/29.10.96/ABU/KENYA/BB.

12   Letter to Stefan Smidt dated 13 November 1996.

Chapter 6

1   'Social Development and Results on the Ground', World Bank's Operations Policy Committee (OPC), September 1996.

2   Nancy Alexander, 'Who Shapes Your Country's Future? A Guide to Influencing the World Bank's Country Assistance Strategies (CASs)', Development Bank Watchers' Project, October 1996.

3   Letter to Roberto Chavez, Resident Representative, World Bank Maputo from Nick Roseveare, Country Representative, Oxfam.

4   Christopher McCrudden, 'Mainstreaming Fairness?', a discussion paper on Policy Appraisal and Fair Treatment, November 1996, Commission for the Administration of Justice, Belfast.

5   Environment Department, 'Social Assessment Structured Learning Preliminary Findings', Dissemination Notes No 37 September 1995, ENVSP World Bank, Washington.

6   John Milimo, Andrew Norton and Daniel Owen, 'The impact of
    PRA approaches and methods on policy and practice: The Zambia
    Participatory Poverty Assessment' (forthcoming article).
7   IDB, *Resource Book on Participation*, Washington, September 1996.
8   Report on Social Policy, May–June 1996, Vol XXIX No 6, NACLA
    Report on the Americas.
9   'Decentralised Planning in Sub-Saharan Africa', FAO Economic and
    Social Development Paper 140, Rome 1997.
10 Ibid.
11 'Democratic and Popular Participation in the Public Field: The
    Experience of the Participative Budget in Porto Alegre (1985–1995)'.
12 Activities in Ceará were based on reforms to State mechanisms
    predicated in the 1988 Constitution, and a raft of progressive social
    legislation which came into force in 1990s, such as the Statute on the
    Child and Adolescent and the Law on Education (1996). The two
    underlying principles of the 1988 Brazilian Constitution are social
    participation and decentralisation. Workshops on participatory
    planning were held, and participatory councils were established at
    municipal and regional level, responsible for the municipalisation of
    sectors like education and agriculture.
13 Carlos M. Vilas, 'Neoliberal Social Policy — Managing Poverty
    (Somehow)', Report on Social Policy, May–June 1996, Vol XXIX No
    6, NACLA Report on the Americas.
14 Jonathan Fox and Josefina Aranda: *Decentralization and Rural
    Development in Mexico: Community Participation in Oaxaca's Municipal
    Funds Programme*, Monograph Series 42, Center for US–Mexican
    Studies, University of California, San Diego, 1996.
15 A newly negotiated project for the afforestation of the Eastern Plains
    of Karnataka will be funded with a large loan from the Japanese
    Overseas Economic and Co-operation Fund. To have any hope of
    success, the programme will need a strong commitment from the
    Japanese to participatory approaches. The Eastern Plains Project
    borrows many of the concepts from DFID's Western Ghats Forest
    Project, but the signs are that KFD will revert to type: its focus is on
    intensive protection of core areas. Despite references to the need to
    involve local people in the planning and implementation of tree-
    planting activity, a reading of the project documents and past
    experience suggest that KFD is likely to make the key decisions on
    zones and impose planting targets on local communities, allowing
    only a token level of participation. If an authoritarian approach is

adopted, it is likely to have a detrimental effect on implementation of the second phase of the Western Ghats project.

16 The World Bank launched the Umidas Strategic Planning Process for Rondônia in August 1997.

17 In June 1996, at a mid-term evaluation workshop held in Porto Velho, the State government, project officials, and the NGO Forum agreed a framework for reformulating the Project.

18 The Bank is still somewhat over-optimistic in its view of the State government, whose development proposals outlined in its two-year action plan run counter to sustainable development objectives. The action plan calls for the paving of some 500km of rural roads ($38mn will come from PLANAFLORO funds). A joint venture with the Brazilian agro-industrial conglomérate, Gruppo Maggi, for the construction of a large grain terminal in Porto Velho was given approval without any EIA being done, although it will have major repercussions on agriculture in the State.

19 EvInfo, 'Project de Gestion et de Conservation de l'Espace Forestier en Ouganda', No 010000.

20 'Policy guidelines for future EU–ACP relations', Commission, 29 October 1997.

21 *The Reality of Aid 1997/8: An Independent Review of Development Co-operation*, Eurostep, ICVA, edited by Judith Randell and Tony German, Development Initiatives, Earthscan, London 1997.

22 Ibid.

23 In October 1997 the British government announced its intention of privatising the Commonwealth Development Corporation to enable it to raise more long-term funding for poorer countries.

24 CDC Development Report, 1996.

25 Business as Partners in Development, Prince of Wales Business Leaders Forum 1996 (in collaboration with the World Bank and UNDP).

Chapter 7

1 'Eliminating World Poverty: A Challenge for the 21st Century', White Paper on International Development, presented to the British Parliament, November 1997.

2 European Commission, 'Policy Guidelines for the Future of EU–ACP Relations ', Brussels, 29 October 1997.

Appendix

1 For more details, see Joan Davidson and Dorothy Myers, *No Time to Waste — Poverty and the Global Environment*, Oxfam UK and Ireland, Oxford, 1992.

2 Estimated at about Rs 181.50 per capita per month in rural areas at 1991 prices.

3 Oxfam's annual budget in Orissa is approximately UK£200,000. In the ten years from 1983/84, ODA's Joint Funding Scheme constituted on average 29 per cent of all Oxfam grants to project partners in Orissa.

4 ODA Evaluation Report, EV 563, 'An Evaluation of Two ODA-Co-funded Oxfam-Supported Projects in Orissa'.

5 Singh 1993.

Selected bibliography

Castells, Manuel, 1997, *The Information Age: Economy, Society and Culture*, Oxford: Blackwell.

Centre for Human Rights Geneva, *Human Rights: A Compilation of International Instruments* (Vol.1, Part 1), 1993, New York: United Nations.

Cernea, Michael M. and Scott E. Guggenheim (eds), 1993, *Anthropological Approaches to Resettlement: policy, practice and theory*, Boulder, Colorado: Westview Press.

Chambers, R., N.C. Saxena, and T. Shah, 1989: *To the Hands of the Poor: Water and Trees*, Oxford and IBH Co. Pvt. Ltd., New Delhi.

Chambers, Robert, 1997, *Whose Reality Counts? Putting the Last First*, London: Intermediate Technology.

Cox, Aidan, John Healey and Antonique Koning, 1997, *How European Aid Works: A Comparison of Management Systems and Effectiveness*, London: Overseas Development Institute.

Edwards, Michael and David Hulme (eds), 1995, *Non-Governmental Organisations — Performance and Accountability*, London: Earthscan and Save the Children.

Fox, Jonathan and Josefina Aranda, 1996, *Decentralization and Rural Development in Mexico: Community Participation in Oaxaca's Municipal Funds Program*, Monograph Series, 42, Center for US-Mexican Studies, University of California, San Diego.

McDowell, Christopher, (ed) 1996, *Understanding Impoverishment, The Consequences of Development Induced Displacement*, Oxford: Berg-Hahn Books.

Rich, Bruce, 1994, *Mortgaging the Earth*, Boston: Beacon Press.

Shihata, Ibrahim F. I., 1994, *The World Bank Inspection Panel*, The International Bank for Reconstruction and Development, New York: Oxford University Press.

Watkins, K., 1995, *The Oxfam Poverty Report,* Oxford: Oxfam (GB).

World Bank, 1989, *Sub-Saharan Africa — From Crisis to Sustainable Growth,* Washington: World Bank.

World Bank, 1996, *Participation Sourcebook,* Washington: World Bank.

Oxfam Insight

Economic Growth with Equity:
Lessons from East Asia

Kevin Watkins

Looks at the lessons to be learned from the phenomenon of economic growth in East Asian countries and whether or not the achievements of the past, in terms of poverty reduction, can be maintained.

ISBN 0 85598 384 1, 1998

Reforming World Trade:
The Social and Environmental Priorities

Caroline LeQuesne

Examines the impact of rapid trade liberalisation on the livelihoods of poor communities and recommends ways in which their rights could be protected.

ISBN 0 85598 346 9, 1996

A Case for Reform:
Fifty Years of the IMF and World Bank

Oxfam Policy Department

Argues that the time has now come for a fundamental review of the policies of the World Bank and the IMF and for a radical reform of their operations.

ISBN 0 85598 301 9, 1995

Also of interest

The IMF, the World Bank, and Economic Policy in Bosnia
David Woodward

Outlines the political and economic situation in Bosnia one year after the end of the war. Identifies the political, economic and social constraints on policy and the consequent dilemmas that face economic policy-makers.

An Oxfam Working Paper
ISBN 0 85598 396 5, 1998

For further details and a complete catalogue of Oxfam publications, please contact:

Oxfam Publishing
274 Banbury Road
Oxford OX2 7DZ, UK

email: publish@oxfam.org.uk
fax: +44 1865 313925

Development in Practice

Editor: Deborah Eade

Development in Practice is a forum for practitioners,
policy-makers, and academics to exchange information
and analysis concerning the social dimensions of development
and humanitarian work. As a multi-disciplinary journal of
policy and practice, *Development in Practice* reflects a wide
range of institutional and cultural backgrounds and a variety
of professional experience.

- Each volume is published in four issues
- Also available in electronic form
- Subsidised subscription rates for developing countries
  available

For further information and to request a sample copy,
please contact:

Carfax Publishing Company
PO Box 25
Abingdon
Oxon
OX14 3UE, UK